IMPROVISE.

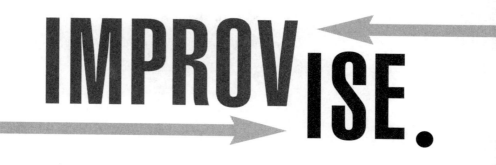

IMPROVISE.

SCENE
FROM THE
INSIDE OUT

MICK NAPIER

HEINEMANN
Portsmouth, NH

Heinemann

361 Hanover Street
Portsmouth, NH 03801–3912
www.heinemanndrama.com

Offices and agents throughout the world

© 2004 by Mick Napier

Library of Congress Cataloging-in-Publication Data
Napier, Mick.
Improvise : scene from the inside out / Mick Napier.
p. cm.
ISBN 0-325-00630-X (pbk. : alk. paper)
1. Improvisation (Acting). I. Title.
PN2071.I5N35 2004
792.02'8—dc22   2003022506

Editor: Lisa Barnett
Production service: Argosy Publishing
Production coordinator: Lynne Reed
Cover design: Night & Day Design
Typesetter: Argosy Publishing
Manufacturing: Steve Bernier

Printed in the United States of America on acid-free paper
16 15 14   VP   15 16 17

For Jennifer Estlin, who is everything to me.

In loving memory of Dr. Martin de Maat, the most inspiring teacher of improvisation the world has ever known.

ontents

Acknowledgments

I would like to thank the following:

Jennifer Estlin, whom I love. Her initial edit of the book prevented me from looking like an idiot. Martin de Maat, the best improv teacher that ever was. My mother, Pat, whom I love and who has been so supportive of this improv roller coaster throughout the years. A big thanks to my brother Mark, the best brother a person could have. My father Fred for his love and humor. Richard and Judy Cohen, Jennifer's wonderful parents. Lyn Pusztai, my dearest friend who makes everything more beautiful. David Combs, my oldest friend. Joyce Sloane—none of us might be improvising if not for her. David MacNerland, who boldly began this improvisational journey with me in college. Gary Hollon, my chess and theater coach in high school. Bill Harbron, my scoutmaster who drove me to be an Eagle. Barbara Bunch, my super-supportive high school Spanish teacher. Papa Romano, who said I should seriously go into acting. Elizabeth Trask, who helped me through some times. Charna Halpern, for creating the Improv Olympic. Josephine Forsberg, for creating The Player's Workshop. Jeffrey Sweet, for writing *Something Wonderful Right Away*. Paul Dinello, Stephen Colbert, Amy Sedaris, David Sedaris, and David Rakoff for inviting me into their bizarre world of creation. Rob Kozlowski, for his referral and support. Christopher Schelling, who was kind enough to help Jennifer and me find our way through the publishing maze. Lisa Barnett, my patient editor and a person who has been enthusiastically supportive from the start.

My Second City friends:

Andrew Alexander, Kelly Leonard, Sheldon Patinkin, Beth Kligerman, Robin Johnson, Alison Riley, Michael Gellman, Ruby Streak, Craig Taylor, and Cheryl Sloane, who gave me my first shot at directing a Second City show. Also, all of the talented actors, musicians, directors, designers, stage managers, and office and wait staff there.

My friends that founded The Annoyance:

Mark Sutton, a talented actor, improviser, teacher, and softball coach. Joe Bill, a tall and talented teacher and improviser. Ellen Stoneking, an amazing writer and actress. Eric Waddell, producer of our first show and game show host. Faith Soloway, the unbelievably talented folk musician. Ed Furman, the funniest man. Susan Messing, who will do anything on stage, and her lovely daughter Sofia Mia. Geoffrey Lantz, who held it together through some rough times.

In addition, I would like to thank *all* of the talented people from The Annoyance past, including David Adler, Tom Booker, Yvonne Bruner, Mike and Beth Coleman, Bob Fisher, Jeff Garlin, Nancy Giangrasse, Dana Goodman, Margueritte Hammersley, Dan Kipp, Richard Laible, Elsa Lajack Keevers, Madeline Long, Bob Morand, Brett Paisle, Eve Pickford, David Razowski, Andy Richter, Al Rose, Scot Robinson, Jill Soloway, Cathy Stanley, Stoley, David Summers, Marisol Torres, Pat Towne, Matt Walsh, Julia Wolov, Ben Zook, and especially Jodi Lennon.

I would also like to thank these additional people in the current Annoyance Ensemble: Lilly Allison, Steve Cowdrey, Sean Cusick, Kyle Dolan, Mark Egmon, Jimmy Fitz, Tom Keevers, Lisa Lewis, Ken Manthey, Lisa McQueen, Tony Mendoza, Peter Renaud, Gary Ruderman, Rebecca Sohn, Rich Sohn, Stan Stankos, Tristan Tamplin, John Terendy and Danielle Montana, Josh Walker, Annie Watson, and Willie.

A special thanks to all the students I've had over all the years.

Lastly, I would like to thank my late pet, Kaluah.

*J*ntroduction

*J*t's strange that I'm writing this book. I wasn't supposed to. Since I was a kid, I've loved math and the sciences. From the time I was in second grade I always knew I would be a veterinarian. "If your dog is sick, just call Mick," was a sign I had always imagined outside of my office.

Then one night in high school I saw a play. I can't remember the name of it, but I do remember the effect it had on me. I knew that although I loved science so much, there was a part of me that wanted to be up there on that stage. I went to that play the very next night, and I was even more astonished. The actors were moving in the exact same places on stage as they had the night before! I had no idea—I thought they just memorized the lines and kind of moved about wherever they wanted—I didn't know it was practiced that much. (While I was in high school, you didn't go to rehearsal; you went to play practice.)

I decided that I wanted to have a go at this thing, so I auditioned. My first role was Grumio, in *The Taming of the Shrew*. I went on to do several more plays in high school, and arrived at Indiana University with a strong desire to be a veterinarian and a conflicting desire to be on stage. It didn't take that long to discover that the latter would win my heart. I began auditioning and performing in play after play, and eventually switched my study to theater. I did indeed love the rush of performing.

Soon, though, I became a little bored. Not with the performing, but with the rehearsing. I felt like the rehearsals were the same thing over and over. I was pretty selfish back then; I wanted the feeling I got when I performed without the repetitious work of the rehearsals. Performing without rehearsals, was there such a thing?

That's when I picked up a book called *Something Wonderful Right Away*, by Jeffrey Sweet. It was a collection of interviews of people involved in something called improvisation. As the title states, you could create something wonderful right away. To me, that meant all the fun without the rehearsing. A friend of mine, David MacNerland, and I decided to form an improv group, never having seen or performed any improvisation. (Maybe David had, I'll have to ask him.) We created a group called "Dubbletaque" and performed for full houses for nearly four years.

Improvisation became my passion, and I moved to Chicago to pursue it.

I studied and performed everywhere I could. It was in this study that I learned for the first time about all of the intricacies of improvisation: forms, rules, scenic structure, and whatnot. It was also at this time that I began to form my own point of view in regard to what makes improvisation work or not. That is in this book. I didn't really know any of this in college, we were just kind of *making it up as we went along.*

So many years later, here I sit. I'm not a veterinarian, although my love for math and science remains to this day. I think you might notice that in this book. Ironically, as a director, I now value the theater and rehearsing more than ever. There's certainly value in something wonderful right away, and an equal yet different value to something wonderful not right away.

This book is for those that have a desire to improvise scenes better. I truly hope it helps.

"If your scene is sick ..."

☑1 What Is Improvisation?

What the hell is improvisation?

Shall I take the long road or the short road?

I'll take the short one—who has time?

Improvisation is getting on a stage and making stuff up as you go along.

That's it.

You didn't know what you were going to say or do and now you find yourself moving about and talking without any real knowledge of what you are going to do next. Amazingly simple, astoundingly difficult—for adults.

Improvisation is used around the globe as a means to write material, a tool in training actors, and as a performance product in and of itself. Improv troupes around the world force reasonably nice people to pay to see the latter. It is for those people that I write this book.

Improv comes in the shape of games (which I won't discuss later), scenes, long forms, monologues, songs, and Freeze Tag. It can be funny on purpose or not funny on purpose. Quite often, unfortunately, it is not funny on not purpose.

I reckon that's what this useless book is all about.

Why useless? Because when it comes down to it, you can read about it until your teeth fall out, but you'll only get better by doing it. Doing it. Doing it.

Given that I truly believe that you'll only get better by doing it, I hope to provide some tricks and guidance to help get you there.

Ready?

2   Rules

*I*f you've ever spent one second in an improv class, you've probably come across The Rules.

I must discuss them first, in order to uncondition your brain. Let's see if I can list a few of them right now.

1. Don't deny.
2. Don't ask questions.
3. Don't dictate action.
4. Don't talk about past or future events.
5. Establish who, what, where.
6. Don't negotiate.
7. Don't do teaching scenes.
8. Show, don't tell.
9. Say "yes," and then say "and."
10. Don't talk about what you are doing.

There are others, but ten is such a pretty number: ten commandments, ten rules—you know.

Rules, rules. A list of rules. Rules of improvisation. There they are, and they're in a list, and they look good, and they even seem to make sense. So why am I so snitty about them? Because I don't believe they work. That is, The Rules do not help one improvise well. As a matter of fact, I believe that they help one not improvise well. They are destructive. And why do I believe this? I will tell you now in excruciating detail.

The History of The Rules

In the beginning, there was an improv scene, and it was good.

In the beginning, there was a good improv scene. It was a miracle. It was playful and vibrant and engaging and funny. It had a whimsical, magical quality that was immeasurable. Those who witnessed it were amazed at what they saw. They said things like, "That was crazy! Those guys will do anything!" and "Oh my God, do you remember when they did this or that?" and "That was funny." Those who performed the miraculous scene stepped off the raised platform astonished. They too were amazed.

It was as if something had taken over their thoughts and actions. They had been imbued with the Spirit of Improvisation. Each word uttered forth was affirmed by the laughter of those who witnessed the scene. It felt good. Trance-like. At its end, they signaled each other with a high-five, a smile, a pat on the shoulder, and a tentative hug. When asked about the scene, later, they replied, "It was cool, it just happened," and "I don't even remember what we did." It was a miracle. It truly was immeasurable.

We laughed, we cried, it was a damn good scene.

As time scrolled on, others attempted to repeat the experience of a good improv scene, but they fell short. Their scene was listless and uninspired. It seemed to go slow.

While they were performing, they really wanted to do something, but for some reason they were rendered immobile. While they were doing the scene, they thought hard about doing it, but nothing seemed to help. The scene grew boring and they knew it. They didn't want it to be boring, but it was.

The longer and harder they thought about it being boring and not being boring, the more it was more and more boring. They were in a trap that they had created and they knew it and they thought about that.

They also thought about how the observers—the audience—must be bored, too, and how they ought to do something right now and they tried to do something but they didn't do anything and that was bad and they thought about that and they thought about thinking about that.

While they were performing the scene they thought even more about what they weren't saying but wanted to say. They thought about wanting to say something smart and fun but they didn't say anything and then they did say something and it was boring and they thought it was stupid and they thought the audience thought it was stupid and they thought about that, too. And then they thought, "OK, now I'm really going to do something," and they didn't, again, and they thought that was bad so they thought about it and realized it wasn't good to be thinking about that, and they thought about that and thought about how they would like to stop thinking about that and they didn't.

Then they thought "It would really be great if the lights went out," and the lights didn't and they thought that was bad. The operator of the lights thought it would be good if the lights went out, too, but couldn't think of a place to stop the scene and kept thinking that something would happen but nothing did, and thought maybe he should take the lights out now anyway and didn't and tried again and didn't and thought that was odd.

Meanwhile, the audience was thinking that they wished the performers would do something and they didn't and the audience thought about how bored and uncomfortable they were.

Finally, after six hours (two minutes), the light person could take no more and really thought he'd better do something so he thought about taking the lights out and he tried and almost did, but didn't and tried again and nearly did, but not, and then he did, and it felt bad and he thought about that but it was over.

The performers didn't think the scene went very well.

Neither did the audience.

It was the first bad improv scene; there were more to follow.

Over time, more and more scenes were improvised, a few good and a lot bad.

The good ones were just good. Oh, they were funny: "Did you see that, wasn't it amazing crazy wow they'll do anything I was laughing so hard don't know why ha ha how do they do that funny funny good time great time ha." The good scenes were beyond measure. They were merely wonderful. Who has time to analyze when you're laughing so hard, and who really wants to? Why bother thinking about something amazing when you just want to sit back and enjoy it? Maybe later you'll analyze the good scene in specific detail by describing it as "amazing," and "crazy," and "out there."

Maybe not.

Maybe magic is best left alone. Maybe.

The bad scenes, however, were not beyond measure. Indeed, they were and are about measure. As a matter of fact, bad improvisation depends on measurement and thinking. In a bad improv scene everyone from the light guy to the audience to the performers themselves is thinking. The audience has time to think because they're so damn bored.

After a while, those who were forced to endure watching innumerous bad improv scenes began to notice things. They were in the mindset to think and analyze so, naturally, critical observation yielded critical results. Patterns of behavior began to emerge in many of the bad improv scenes they watched.

It seemed that in many of the bad improv scenes the participants often denied the reality of the other player. One player would bring forth a plausible truth regarding the location or the players' relationship to one another and the other player would refute that reality.

In other bad improv scenes, the players would ask fruitless questions that seemed to stifle the action and prevent the scene from moving forward.

Often a boring scene would have one of the players merely telling the other player what to do, or talk about events in the past and/or in the future.

Several of the "when will this be over" scenes took place in an ambiguous location with ambiguous activities and relationships.

In the middle of potentially good scenes, one of the players would often begin to negotiate the sale of a good or service, or partake in teaching the other player a skill.

Still other bad scenes relied on talking about a subject, instead of portraying that activity as if it were happening at present in that locale. Some players in bad scenes went so far as to merely talk about what they were doing.

These things, and others, were attributes observed in the bad, boring, "when will the lights go out?" scenes.

Yep indeedy, there was truly a correlation between a bad improv scene and certain specific behavioral attributes. Most boring scenes contained at least one if not more of these patterns. Time after time these patterns were confirmed, as more and more people shared the observation. And as is often the case, when a phenomenon is observed repeatedly, a hypothesis is formed:

Certain observed patterns of behavior = bad scene.

"It seems that every time a bad improv scene happens, the same patterns of behavior show up. So, perhaps, if we could just get rid of the bad behavior, a good scene will materialize."

Another hypothesis was formed:

Not certain observed patterns of behavior = mysterious good scene.

"If we can get the improvisers to stop behaving that way, then surely a good scene will emerge!"

If we can get them to stop asking questions the scene will move forward. Tell them not to deny and they will be proactive. No more teaching scenes or negotiating beats or dictation of action or talking about future or past events and then, yes then, (yes and) then, a good scene will show up. If you eliminate the bad, the good will magically appear.

"Let us accumulate a list of these negative behavioral patterns and announce them."

We shall call these The Rules of improvisation.

· Seems to make sense. Seems to make sense.

Problem. Problem.

The problem is that the hypothesis is untrue.

Yes, there is a correlation between bad scenes and specific behavior, but it is not causal. The behavior is consequential. Scenes that are bad to begin with often yield such behavior, but the behavior itself does not cause the scene to be bad. Correlation does not necessarily equal causality. There is a correlation between objects released from the top of buildings and objects that fall to the ground, but the buildings do not cause the object to fall, gravity does. (Or warped space if you take a relativistic view.)

One might notice that when the sales of bicycles increase, so does the number of boating accidents. Does riding bicycles cause boating accidents? No, there's a third variable that causes both. It's called summer.

Something else causes boring scenes, but often boring scenes show up with the behavior that eventually shaped The Rules of improvisation.

(So what causes a bad improv scene? That's for later.)

The ironic thing about all of this is that the literal bad moves noticed in bad scenes show up nearly as often in wonderful scenes. (Scenes with wonder: I wonder why they work?)

That is to say, in great scenes there are many questions and players telling stories of the past and whatnot, but they go largely unnoticed. People are usually too busy laughing or being in awe to notice such things: just havin' fun, you know. Every once in a while a question or the word "no" is caught by someone watching a good scene, and it's chalked up as an exception, with little further explanation.

Maybe someday you'll be good enough to break a rule and be an exception.

Maybe this afternoon.

Now for even more fun.

Not only do I believe that the aforementioned behavior (that which does not adhere to The Rules) does not cause bad scenes, I do believe that the teaching of "behavior that adheres to The Rules" can cause bad scenes. My hypothesis would read:

Learning rules can cause bad improvisation.

Why, why?

Because the worst part about rules is that people remember them. Often above and beyond anything else. It satisfies and stimulates the left brain. Oh, for a list. "There they are, all numbered and listed. I can remember that. I will remember that. I will remember The Rules

of improvisation. How could I not? After all, they are The Rules."
They stick to the brain like glue. They help you think about stuff.
Why, you can't help but think about The Rules. They're all memorized in your head. They're "in your head." ("Excuse me, how do I get
'out of my head'?") The Rules, The Rules: got 'em all? Think about
them, 'cause you don't want to break one, think long and hard—

Now improvise, play!

Good luck.

Yes. That's why I'm not a big fan of The Rules. They help people
think in a particular way, and that way of thinking is often death to
good improvisation. I've watched those damn Rules screw people up
for years, and I don't mean that for years, I've seen The Rules screw
people up. Individuals who can think of nothing else on stage but
The Rules, wandering around powerlessly, for years, thinking and
measuring and being very careful not to break The Rules, all the
while wondering why they are not improving. Improvising.

Left brain analytical heaven. Not very much fun.

Not much fun to be on stage wanting to do something, all the
while thinking about not doing something, such as asking a question. No good time in wanting to listen to your partner while
thinking about not teaching her. Little power in wanting to break out
with a wild character and not quite doing so because you're thinking
about not talking about an event in the future.

What's more, I've seen hundreds of scenes that don't violate any
of The Rules of improvisation that make me yearn for naptime. What
the . . . ? Scenes that engage in all of The Rules of improvisation and
the scenes are still boring as hell?

Oh yeah, believe you me:

*Proper execution of The Rules in an improv scene does not necessarily
yield a good improv scene.*

Furthermore,

*Not breaking any of The Rules does not necessarily yield a good improv
scene.*

Rules themselves are irrelevant to good improvisation, but
thinking about them is not.

Fear Fear Fear

Whether irrelevant or not, the behavior exhibited in bad scenes exists.

Where does this behavior come from? Why do bad scenes always seem to show up with the same observable patterns?

Fear fear confusion confusion fear think think think—fear.

Each day we adult humans walk around just trying to get through the day. How the heck do we do it? We protect ourselves. Our consciousness. Our thinking. We can think, we can choose, and we can act based on that choice. That's what we humans do. Early humans began to remember things and make choices based on what they memorized. It was to their advantage to do so. I can imagine the mind of a human habilis five million years ago, thinking, "Hmmm, every time I go down that path that other guy throws a rock at my head and calls my woman names. Today, having remembered that information, I will go down this other path to get home to the tree."

It was an advantage for this guy to remember this information and act on it. Those that had this selective advantage survived over those that did not. Those that remembered not to go down that path didn't get rocks thrown at their heads and survived better. Those that didn't remember went down that path and, sure enough, got a rock thrown at their head. They eventually died off, so consciousness survived as the natural selective advantage. We humans think, so we survive better. Humans who think well survive better than those who do not. We constantly protect ourselves and advance ourselves with our ability to think. We rely on it for everything.

If, as a child, I break the garage window, I must think of exactly what I'm going to say to Mom so that she will protect me from Dad. If I'm going to ask Mary to the prom, I must think about what I'm going to say in order to protect myself from appearing foolish and to succeed in obtaining the date. If I want to get the job, I must consider the interview beforehand and think of every possible question I could be asked and every possible answer I can provide. If I am to present a sales proposal, I must carefully consider all possible objections and think about how to overcome them.

It has been the same thing for millions of years. People fear things so they think of ways to prevent an unwanted outcome.

So what the hell does this have to do with improvisation? I'll surely tell you now.

Improvisers carry seven million years of human consciousness on stage with them every time they improvise a scene. And they do what humans should do, the thing that humans do in every other situation in their lives: They carefully consider all possible scenarios and think about what they will do so that they will remain safe and do and say the appropriate things.

This kind of thinking is what has become known in improv land as "in your head." It's a measured way of thinking that has one consider, stop, reconsider, think, look, stop, consider, okay, think, stop, think, consider, wait, stop, think, etc.

Unfortunately, good improvisation has nothing to do with safety or appropriateness. (As a matter of fact, it's quite the opposite.)

When this way of thinking is brought into the improv scene, the audience and the performers alike soon discover that it is boring. The audience didn't pay two dollars to see adult humans think and consider options around them. That's what they watch and participate in all dull-day-long. They want to see people play and play hard. Throw caution (thinking) to the wind (out). Really play.

If improvisers aren't truly playing then they are "thinking about." If fear has them thinking in this way at the beginning of the scene, they are sure to discover that their scene is boring from the audience's perspective. The consequence of that realization is more fear and confusion. That is to say, when the scene starts to go awry, and the performer and audience alike both discover this early on, the improviser gets scared and confused. What do human adults do when they are scared and confused?

Defend and protect.

When in a situation that is scary and confusing, human adults will often ask questions in order to get information to protect themselves. They may seek false power by dictating action to others, or seek manufactured status by teaching others how to do something and/or by saying no to another's proposal or idea. One who is scared and confused might try to gain control of her situation by justifying who she is, what she's doing, and where she's doing it. One who is frightened to do something right now may recount a past event, or talk about an event that may happen in the future, or negotiate a proposition. One that terrified may even desperately attempt to figure out what's going on so much, he literally starts talking about what he is doing.

Fear begets thinking.

Thinking begets protective behavior.

Protective behavior is noticed as patterns in bad improvisation.

Patterns of behavior become rules.

The Rules of improvisation: remember them well.

Breaking The Rules

"Don't you have to know The Rules first before you can break them?"

I've been asked that question a few hundred times. It's usually a student who has already spent $2,658 on improv classes. (People like to justify their expenses.) I wish I could provide comfort, but unfortunately the answer is "No."

I do not believe one must learn The Rules in order to break them.

Why learn how not to do something in lieu of learning how to do something? Why improvise with the baggage of inactive thinking?

In electricity, if I learned and practiced how *not* to wire an outlet, I would die. In skydiving, if I learned and practiced how *not* to open a parachute, I would die. In lion taming—you get my contrived point.

Well, I've seen many a scene die with the thinking and practice of The Rules. Why not learn how to improvise and let the negative behavior associated with The Rules disappear as a consequence?

Again, in the form of an equation:

Adherence to The Rules does not equal a good scene.
Thinking about The Rules can equal a bad scene.
The Rules of improv are irrelevant to good improv.

If so, then why do The Rules persist in improv training decade after decade?

I wish I had an answer to that. Oh, as a matter a fact I do.

First, because as I stated before, The Rules seem to make sense. In an awful scene, The Rules look like the reason the scene is bad, so it seems logical to dwell on them.

Second, good scenes are a drag to talk about and many people wouldn't even know what to say. I've seen soooo many instructors watch a bad scene and chalk it up to "too many questions" or "talking in the future." I've seen as many, after a good scene, say (with a half-laugh), "Great, that's how it's done, two more."

That's how *what's* done?

I can't really blame them though. It makes sense to discuss The Rules in regard to a bad scene, but it doesn't feel right to break down a great scene. Students and teachers alike love to satisfy their left brain and analyze that which failed, but nobody likes to mess with magic.

How to Improvise

Part One: Do Something!

For God's sake, do something. Anything. Something. At the top of an improv scene, do something. Please, do it for yourself. Do yourself a favor and just do something.

You see, there's this guy you know, nice enough fellow, and he's always talking about what he's going to do someday. He has big plans, and if he's in The Business, then he talks about a screenplay he's gonna write or a thing he's going to shoot on video or an idea he has for an improv form. If he's not in The Business then he talks about what he's gonna do at work or to his house or some scheme he has for this or that. He talks endlessly in great detail of the necessary steps he will take to someday execute his master plan for whatever he will do and speaks of all of the rewards he will gain once he does this thing.

Maybe you know this guy for two or three years and begin to notice that he doesn't really carry out anything he talks about doing. Perhaps you begin to label him as a "talker" or "full of it." Maybe as he speaks of his next scheme you begin to think to yourself, "I wish this guy would stop talking about it and just do it."

And as time goes by, you see this guy at parties and notice that you are doing a little bit to avoid him. When he catches you and engages you in conversation, you begin to observe that you are bored with his "someday I will do this" tirade. As a matter of fact, you start looking around the room at other people kinda hoping someone will rescue you from this person because you are so bored. There he is again talking about something he's gonna do, and you know that it's never gonna happen and it bores the hell out of you to have to listen to it again.

Two weeks later he catches you walking down the street and now, as he approaches, you actually get a little angry on the inside. You're still nice but you feel as if your time is being wasted. You want nothing more than to release yourself from this guy who never does anything but talks endlessly about what he's going to do someday. You wish he would just do something, anything, and stop talking about it.

This is the way your audience feels when you don't do something in an improv scene. They are bored, distracted, and a little angry that someone who isn't doing anything is wasting their time.

You're not like the guy above, though, who is talking out loud about doing something and then not doing it. No, your conversation is silent; it's all in your head. That's where the talking is going on. For the audience, though, it may as well be out loud. They still have to wait for the conversation to be over. They are still waiting and thinking, "I wish somebody would do something." They don't give a damn what you are thinking about, they just want you to do something. They, the audience, don't even require a specific thing that they want you to do. They just want you to do something— anything. "Please, somebody do something." They don't even know what "do something" means. They only know that nothing is going on and they are bored and have been given the opportunity to think and that the thing they are thinking is, of course, "Do something."

Perhaps, in that scene, you are thinking the same thing.

But what do I do?

Who gives a damn? *That* you do something is far more important than *what* you do.

At the top of an improv scene, in the first crucial moments, it is far more important that you do something than what it is you actually do. And why is this? Why is it important to give little credence to what you do as long as you do something at the top of an improv scene? I will tell you:

It will snap you out of your head.

And that's half the battle. It will allow you to make a choice out of power as opposed to fear. It will eliminate the mere two seconds (or less) that it will take you to start talking yourself out of the scene. It will put you in a "I don't know what I'm doing but I'm doing it anyway" mode of being. This is the first step to playing, and it's powerful and fearless and bold and *un*apologetic, and it has you start a scene "out of your head," which is, of course, the best way to stay out of your head. It makes that sudden snap and jolt to the irrational, where good improvisation is housed, and allows you to . . .

Take care of yourself first!

At the top of an improv scene, in the very beginning, take care of yourself first. That's right, be very selfish at the top of your scene. Do something, anything for yourself first. You'll have plenty of time to "support your partner" later.

Too many scenes have gone to hell because at the very beginning of a scene an improviser thinks about their partner first. And what do they actually do? They may stare at their partner with a glass in their hand and say "So," or "Hey," waiting for and allowing their partner to initiate the scene. Your partner may be doing the same thing, being courteous and allowing you to make the first move. Maybe they say, "What's up?"

Two people on stage staring at each other and wondering who's going to make the first move. Two people being nice to each other and allowing the other to start doing something. In that short amount of time, two humans have created themselves as powerless and thinking entities who are waiting for one or the other to do something, all in the name of courteousness and/or support for their partner. Who has time? The audience is waiting. They don't care about your support. They care about what you do. What you do now.

The grand irony is that the times I've felt most supported in an improv scene is when my partner took care of herself first. When my fellow player selfishly makes a choice, any choice, at the top of the scene, I feel very supported. I feel supported because now I'm on stage with a powerful, playful person who isn't afraid to take a chance. I'm on stage with a fearless individual, and not someone in her head, rendered speechless by fear, and waiting for me to do something.

I feel very supported by power, very unsupported by fear.

The best thing you can do to support me in an improv scene is to take care of your own deal first. If you don't take care of yourself, how the hell are you going to take care of me?

(Still seem selfish? Of course, that's why we'll revisit this later.)

Making that strong move at the top also allows you to . . .

Declare a position in the scene.

Declare a position. Simply, selfishly take a position in the scene. What does this mean?

It could mean a lot of things; it's all in the context of just doing something. It doesn't even have to involve words. It's just, what is your *deal*? What's your deal going to be in the scene? What card are you going to play? Every scene has a deal. Some people say this is "What the scene is about" or "The game of the scene."

Every great scene you can think of—improv or written—has a *deal*: what it's about, a game, what it's centered in, etc. Often that comes with the converging points of view of each improviser.

The points of view could be in agreement or not; it's irrelevant. Maybe it's that your character speaks in one-word responses, or inflects upward at the end of a sentence, or is jealous of everything, or hops when he speaks, or sings or hits herself every time something is asked of her.

Maybe it's just a slice-of-life character scene, in which the respective deals are the characters themselves. Whatever. It doesn't matter; it could be anything.

Your deal is your personal road map for the scene.

Your deal is your guide and you create it. Whatever it is (and it just doesn't matter what), it has a far better chance of emerging as a result of a bold choice at the very top of the scene than it does if you wait for it.

It's all still just playing, but what are you going to play with when you play? You have to create it, but what it is doesn't matter. That's the tricky part. Initiating something for yourself, not caring about what it is, realizing the power of just doing it and catching up with what you did later.

It defies logic. It is fun. And most of all—

It's exciting for the audience.

It doesn't leave them waiting for you to do something someday. It catches them off guard and tells them that this isn't going to be one of those scenes where we ease into it and think through it. A strong declaration at the top tells them that you are ready and there's no time to think. No time for them, and no time for you.

That's exciting. That's vital. That's strong. That's playful.

I remind you, when we were kids we didn't think about how we were going to play or what we were going to do, we just made a move and caught up with it later.

"So when the lights come up, do I scream?"

No. You may, but you certainly don't have to.

When I say *anything*, I mean anything. Quite often when we speak of *power* and *bold* and *immediacy*, we think of *frenetic* and *loud energy*. It doesn't have to be. The snap I speak of in the beginning of the scene can come in many forms. It could be a quiet "Hmmm" or a subtle observation or a word or a shift in body weight. It is literally anything.

You'll know when you've made a move and created something for yourself. You'll know when it feels good and you've snapped into something. You might be a little scared, but you won't care in a wonderful way. And that's a world of difference.

Here I am, describing the indescribable. Just know that declaring your position in a scene is a move to protect yourself first. It doesn't even have to involve words; it could be anything.

A Word About No Words

Be careful. Too many improvisers don't say something at the top of a scene not out of choice, but out of fear. And while it's true that probably only one improviser will initiate the scene with words, it doesn't hurt for you to condition yourself to do so.

Words are the scary part of improvisation. In the words you will reveal your sense of humor, your intelligence, your values, etc. You will have many wonderful silent scenes as well, but scenes with words will dominate.

Whether something we say will be perceived as funny/intelligent/clever is what gets us in our heads most of the time.

The more importance you place on what you say, the more you will think about it, and the less you will be able to say words that are funny/intelligent/clever. Quite the contrary, when you spend your time thinking about talking, what eventually does come out of your mouth is quite stupid, nearly prehistoric.

If you've been in a scene and afterward you felt like an idiot, like you said stuff you would never say in real life, I'll bet my pocket watch you spent a great deal of time in the scene thinking about saying, or thinking about what to say, or thinking of something to say and then deciding not to, and you got to a point where you felt like you had to say something, and what you produced was stupid.

So, if after all that thinking what you come up with is so awful, you might as well say anything right off the top, even if you don't know what you're saying. And most of the time it's not what you say anyway, it's how you say it. More on that later.

Make sense? I hope not.

Grabbing an Object at the Top of the Scene
Grabbing an object at the top of an improv scene can be a wonderful thing, and it can also be a death sentence.

I was told by many to go to my environment—to grab an object at the beginning of the scene. And in my pleading with you to just do anything, grabbing an object certainly qualifies. Then why the possible death sentence? It's how you grab the object.

Oh, listen carefully.

If there's nothing behind (not anything behind) reaching for and holding that object, then it's merely a stall so you can think more.

I'll say it again.

Sometimes going for an object right off the top is great, but sometimes it's an extension of thinking your way through a scene.

Six million and three times I have watched improvisers reach for the obligatory object and stand there and hold it while they think of something to say for twenty-three seconds. They did do something at the top, but there was nothing going on, no deal. That's why I stress the *how*.

The lights come up: An improviser grabs a pointer, aims at a blackboard with a sneer and says in a British accent, "Interesting notion." Another scene, another improviser. Lights up: The improviser grabs a cup, looks at it, looks at her partner, looks at the cup again, and after eight seconds comes up with "So, how's it going?" It's the difference between the sun and Pluto.

The first improviser had something going on. Even if he didn't know where he was going, the object was an integral part of the scene's initiation. The second improviser grabbed her object as a crutch (and often it really is a cup), and held it while she continued to think about what her partner was doing and what she was going to say, etc. I would rather improvise my scene with the first improviser.

An object at the top can be a wonderful tool, or a horrible safety, depending on how you use it in your initiation.

Preconceiving Ideas
"Can I think of the 'anything' I'm going to initiate before the scene starts?"

Or, in other words, is it okay to preconceive an idea in an improv scene? Is it okay to be backstage thinking of something you are going to bring to a scene before you get a suggestion or before the lights come up?

My possibly surprising answer to these questions is a qualified yes.

I say yes because I know that improvisers are going to do it anyway. Is it cheating? In the empirical sense, yes, it probably is. If improvisation is truly grabbing a suggestion from an audience (or not), and truly making it up as you go along, then I suppose preconceiving an idea is defying the pure improv scene. But, like I said, you're probably going to do it more than once (I know I have), so there may as well be an honest discussion about it.

First of all, let me see if I can list the different shades involved in the preconception of an improv initiation.

- Someone who thinks of all the beats of the scene beforehand and attempts to force their partner into their scenario
- Someone who thinks of a "funny" line and decides that they'd like to sway the scene in a way that will allow them to get that line in
- Someone who chooses a favorite character, no matter what the suggestion, that has worked in the past
- Someone who chooses an emotional state, such as "I'm going to be sad in this scene."

- Someone who creates a first line beforehand and executes that line at the start of the scene

I think these are all the things one could do before and as the scene begins. Let's honestly take these one by one and see if we can see what works best. I'll offer a little observation/opinion of each.

Preconceiving the Beats

A pitfall of many beginning improvisers: They come up with a grand idea, an actual arrangement of beats, and attempt to manipulate the scene to fit those beats. This is an extreme burden on the improviser and his victim, the partner in the scene. In this method, one is attempting to weigh every possible variable in the scene and adapt it to the beats in his head. It is rarely successful, if success equals having an interesting and/or funny scene. Too much left-brain baggage to bring to a scene.

Actually, I don't know if it's ever been successful because I don't think it's ever really been done, not at least without a discussion with the partner beforehand—and even then it's a *huge* roll of the dice. Too many things happen in a scene. It's silly to try to improvise a scene while remembering beats, educate your partner to these beats, maintain a character, adapt the beats to the audience suggestion and given location, force your partner to go down the path you've chosen, and all the while make it look like you're "making it up on the spot."

Why bother?

Beginning improvisers do this because they really need the left-brain control before they improvise. They feel they need the safe construct of a preconceived idea. Those who are new to improv also haven't yet learned that improvisation's success does not lie in premise, but in the audience's perception of relationship created through point of view or character or some other deal.

Preconceived beats: Practice this, and you are practicing the devil's work.

Forcing a Funny Line

Have fun. While the improviser is busy thinking of how to find a way to say that line, there's a scene going on. If she is successful at some point in blurting out the line, it's usually inappropriate and sticks out like a sore thumb and is the opposite of very funny.

Using a Character That Always Works For You

This is done all the time. There's a well of characters each improviser has and they use them because they know they will always get laughs. And they do—for a while. Soon the well runs dry. Soon could be two months or five years, depending on the improviser. The characters are still in the well, but for some reasons the laughs go away.

This is a very common middle phase for improvisers.

Character energies start to lose steam. Things that always worked now rarely do. In this phase something quite interesting happens to improvisers. They either decide that they are not very good and leave improvisation, or they persevere and learn that improvisation is not about executing five good characters on a regular basis, but deciding that one does not have a finite "number" of characters. The well is not empty after all. It contains an infinite number of characters. These characters are based on every life experience they've ever had, everything they feel about the world, and everything they've ever seen. Improvisers only have to do anything in the beginning of the scene, and those characters will find them. Then a world opens up and improvisers no longer think of the few characters they rely on, but think of themselves as improvisers who can do, or at least try, any character. Strange thing—after a while those first five characters usually show up again in their improvisation, but now they are much more vital and funny because they are not used out of safety but out of novel, powerful choice.

Choosing an Emotional State Beforehand

I don't mind this one.

An emotional state suggests nothing of the content of the scene. If any emotional state is as good as another and it doesn't affect logistical considerations in the scene, then why not? It, as everything, depends on the context in which the improviser is choosing the emotion.

If you are getting ready to do a scene and you decide to play that sad person that you always play successfully, then you're probably no better off than in the previous example (prechoosing a character).

If you decide you're going to play the scene angry because you'll have more control, then you risk the same traps as in the examples of preconceiving beats/lines.

Maybe you always choose an emotion because you're afraid to do otherwise. Then you're improvising from a construct of safety and it isn't the most powerful position you can be in.

If, on the other hand, you are doing a long form and notice that you've played three scenes in a row where you've been the "laughing guy," and decide to create variety with a different emotional state, then good for you and good for the show.

Or if you notice that you have found yourself in a rut playing angry energies and decide that you want to grow as an improviser with another choice, then really good for you. If you have to think of something to do before you improvise a scene, an emotional state is pretty harmless and wide open and can be a powerful starting point. Depends on why you're choosing it.

Thinking of a Line to Start the Scene

All humans who are or who have improvised have done this. I certainly have. I don't know anyone who hasn't. So am I saying that everyone who has ever improvised in the history of improvisation has done this at one time? Yes, yes I am.

It would be great if all scenes were as pure as the driven snow but they are not.

Improvisers do think of lines before their scenes; I seek to look at how they do that. If an improviser thinks of the line, "I am a robot and you are my robot father and together we are going to eliminate humans so that our brothers and sisters from the Andromeda Galaxy can take over the planet and our leader is on our space phone now, so why don't you talk to him and tell him more about the plan while I watch," then there is probably trouble a-brewin'. Too much information; little room for discovery in the scene. A lot more power would come from a sad, "So, you're here."

Unfortunately, it takes a while for an improviser to get this. It also takes a while for an improviser to learn how to execute a first line without it appearing contrived and preconceived. Even if you become proficient at presenting that first line, you have to become as proficient at letting it go if your partner initiates the scene and it doesn't quite fit into the contextual scheme of the line in your head.

Oh, you'll learn to respond to the initiation while keeping the flavor of your first line intact and sometimes it will even look "improvised." Over time, you'll learn that dropping your preconception is as good as adapting it to the initiation, and then, if you're lucky, you'll learn that not having a first line at all is as, if not more, effective than having a preconceived first line in the first place.

In an improv scene it is far more important *that* you do something than *what* you do.

Part Two: Check Out What You Did.

After you do something at the top of the scene, after you've made a real choice, take half a second to check out what you did. Immediately after you do something, assess what you created.

Let's say the lights came up on stage and you look out over the audience and without thinking, yawn and initiate the line, "Ah, Saturdays." That's a start of an improv scene. You've succeeded in the first step: You took care of yourself by initiating and you had something going on behind it (seemingly bored or tired as evidenced by the yawn—it's something).

Now what?

Now what the hell do you do? The lights came up and you are improvising and you said "Ah, Saturdays." What do you do now? I'll tell you what some improvisers do. Some improvisers might think, "Why did I say that?" or "What's my partner doing now?" or "What am I going to say next?" or "That was boring," or "Why did I say it's Saturday?" or "Why am I looking out over the audience, is this a window?" or "That didn't work," or a host of other things like that. Sometimes by the time the improviser has gone through those thoughts the partner is responding in the scene, or already did.

So what am I suggesting? This.

To chill out and merely check out what you did—in a real literal way. Like, "Oh, I just said 'Ah, Saturdays' kinda' bored and I'm looking out." That's it. That's all. Period. No speculation, no self-judgment, no seeking answers to questions, no worrying about what ifs. Merely assessing what you literally created. "What did I just do? Oh."

Why, why, why?

Because you've just created your character's road map to the scene. That's where it lies. The move you just made. In what you just did. That's where the deal is for you and your character. The very first thing you said or did from your character's point of view lies in that moment, and I'm asking you to take one half second to merely check out what that was. What did you literally just create? Oh that, very well.

A lot of improvisers create something at the top of the scene and have no idea what the hell they just created. I've seen it so many times and so have you.

An improviser will say something at the top of a scene, the very first line, and get a laugh. After the laugh subsides, that improviser says something else. The second line lies flat. It's disappointing to the audience and God. In fact it's almost anger-invoking, because it's obvious from the improviser's second line that he didn't get the deal behind his first line; that is, he didn't know what he was doing.

Literally, such improvisers do not know-what-they-*are*-do-ing.

Create boldly in the first moment, then check out what's up.

Good improvisers do this without even realizing it sometimes. It's automatic. Make an intuitive self-appraisal that has nothing to do with worrying or wondering what is going to happen next. Merely that you did something and what it was.

Notice there is no *why* in that statement.

Who cares why you did something? Most of the time in improvisation asking (or answering) why you did or said a particular thing is a form of judgment and measurement that will get you in your head. It's only important that you did it.

How about *how*? Yes, yes.

How is everything in improvisation. How people do something in improvisation is most of the reason people laugh at improvisation. The line "Goat is good eatin'" may or may not be funny in and of itself. But did you say it as a southerner, someone bored, someone who stutters, someone who's scared, someone who jumps every time they say a sentence, someone with a nervous tic? How, how, how?

Words are of little impact when not filtered through the *how*. The how comprises everything from emotion to state of being to character to character attribute to intonation to physical score to point of view. The how is your deal in the scene, the magical road map for the character, created instantaneously, acknowledged there-after, and played, I said played, furiously.

Part Three: Hold on to What You Did.

Hold on to what you acknowledged yourself doing and how you did it, and do it more, in every way possible and at every opportunity. Do not let go, and passionately make more of it. Be possessed with what you created and how you are doing it.

In *The Wizard of Oz*, Dorothy must passionately hold on to the notion of going back to Kansas. *How* she does this is *in an innocent way.* She must never waver from that innocent desire. She can have lots of things happen to her in that scenario—poppy fields, witches, and flying monkeys—but her innocent desire must grow stronger and stronger. The Tin Man must always want a heart, the Lion courage, and the Scarecrow a brain. They must never change, for if they do the movie's all but over.

This is all so true in improvisation, as well. The only difference is that you are creating the entire Dorothy on the spot.

It is perhaps the trickiest part of improvisation: Hanging on to what we create and heightening it, or making more of it. There are a few reasons I believe this is hard for people.

- We're too nice.
We have a belief that by driving our point of view home in a scene we are railroading our fellow player. This belief might be true if you didn't use simple give-and-take communication and yelled continu-ously. But simply holding on to your creation and heightening it is not rude, it's expected! Good improvisers want their partners to create a powerful character or point of view and stick to it—not for them to tiptoe around and be polite and fizzle their character and give in. In improvisation, this kind of nice is not nice, it's weak.

- We reach our fear threshold.
We go for a bit on a particular trek, fear we can't go anymore, and give in on our point of view by apologizing for it or by saying we were just kid-ding or by many other ways I'll chirp about later. You feel like what you are doing isn't working and won't work so you find a way to give up.

- We think we've run out of things to do.
"There's no way I can keep finding ways to exhibit this character and its point of view in the scene. All the possibilities are exhausted."

All I can say to that is that the possibilities are endless. You could improvise for an hour with that character if you had to. I know because I've seen and done it. When improvisers do the same thing over and over in a scene and feel locked in that thing, all they think is, "This isn't working, I'd better try something else." It's the something else that is key. Instead of changing your entire character and its point of view, create something else in the scene the character can react through. I say *through* and not *to*, because everything in an improv scene must be filtered through characters.

- We think that different is funny.
Beginning improvisers often think that different is funny. "Must always be different, do something different. If I create this one character, it must change its mind all the time, or change the reality, or deny the reality, or question the partner's behavior, and that's what will be funny." Ouch. The funny of improvisation comes from the choices one makes as a character in the relationship with another character, not switching up the character or relationship or the partner.

Always hold on to the thing that you discover you created. Hell, you created it, so hold on to it for dear life. Not only hold on, but also heighten it and exploit it for all it is worth.

Dorothy wants to get back to Kansas. But she can't stand around singing "Over the Rainbow" for two hours. She has to get on the yellow brick road and experience some wild and exciting adventures along the way. No matter the interesting obstacle, she must filter the experience through her unwavering desire to get home and her undying innocence.

Same with improvisation, but you create your own Dorothy, yellow brick road, witches, and flying monkeys, never talking about why there's a road or even an Oz, just accepting and experiencing it, never ever giving up your desire to get home to Kansas, and never ever defiling your innocence.

That is the *play* in improvisation. Creating a thing out of thin air, acknowledging what it is and *how* it does what it does, making bold choices from within that thing, and filtering everything else that comes your way through it, as well.

The Magic of Improvisation

The magic of improvisation doesn't happen because you did or did not follow rules.

Perhaps you've already experienced it. Either by choice or happenstance, I'll bet you had a great character that couldn't say a word without getting affirmation from the audience (usually a laugh).

You were in a zone, totally out of your head, and hitting every line and action. What you were doing, if you think about it (it's hard to because it was a good scene), is improvising from a character or point of view that was never violated (you didn't bail) but was exploited for all it was worth. Everything that came out of your mouth was funny because it was filtered through that character or disposition you created. It feels like magic. It was really your choice at work. Something you created. Something you recognized. And something you played.

◢◣ 4 ◢◣ "What About My Partner?"

At this point, what I've described may appear to be a very selfish way to improvise.

Improvisers are told, "Support your partner" from the moment the scene starts and throughout. I know I was always told that, from the very first improv class I ever took. And here I have you creating something for yourself first and then assessing what it is and holding on to your own initiation and heightening it.

Where does the partner come in?

What happened to all that feel-good improv support? It looks like you are taking care of yourself first. Indeed, that is exactly what I recommend.

Take Care of Yourself First.

If the first thought in your head when you approach an improv scene is "Support your partner" and that's what you hold to be most important, then I ask . . .

What are you supporting them with?

Are you supporting them with thoughts about supporting them? That's very nice but not very supportive. It's so easy to say, "Support your partner." I've heard it for years: "Make your partner look good." But what the hell does it mean? Do you say nice things to them, do you uber-agree, do you pat them on the head, offer them a chair, rub their shoulders? No, the most supportive thing you can do is get over your pasty self and selfishly make a strong choice in the scene. Then you are supporting your partner with your power, and not your fear.

If you want to support your partner in an improv scene, give them the gift of your choice. I only feel supported by my partners if they make a move, if they do something. If they just stand there and look at me thinking about supporting me, I am absolutely unsupported. The more powerful a choice they make, the more I am supported.

"Support your partner" is a two-penny phrase that quite often makes improvisers weak. It's in the realm of "Isn't improvisation a nice nice fantasy land where everyone is magical and nice and supportive?"

That's all nice. But it makes for improvisation where people constantly acquiesce their power and never make a move.

I'll say it again.

You want to support your partner? Do something now.

They'll feel supported, believe me. They will also be grateful. No one likes weak pandering, especially your audience.

Two people making strong choices is nothing but supportive.

After a great scene, improvisers don't feel wonderful because they were in the scene thinking the words "Support my partner." They were in the space they created, listening to their partner and filtering every word or action response through the character or point of view.

Another way you can support your partner is to keep your own choice intact once you've made it. Adhere to and heighten the character or point of view that you have created. You do neither yourself nor your partner good if you create something and then switch up, bail, change your mind out of fear, or drop an initiation you've made in the scene. Stick to the powerful choice you have created and you will most definitely support your partner.

Take Care of Your Partner.

"What about my partner's function in the scene, how can I support that?"

God bless. What about your partner's creation?

First of all, nobody's function arrives by magic. It is the result of the choices made by all parties on stage. Your partner's function is all that they initiate and all that they respond to in response to your choices.

Both functions are mutually carved through a series of (hopefully) powerful choices.

Points of view arrive as a result of these choices, and thus form what the scene is about, or the relationship, or the game of the scene, all of which are quite often the same things.

For example, as a result of your choices (or choices you have both made) in the scene, your partner's character is angry at your character (let's say your character is laughing at him). You can support your partner's point of view by making him angrier, thereby adding fuel to the fire of your partner's point of view and helping him to heighten his character. Most of the time though, you are doing this by simultaneously heightening your own point of view (your character laughs at everything your partner's character does).

The more your character laughs at everything his character does, the angrier your partner's character becomes. That is the relationship of this scene. That is what this scene is about. That is the game of this scene. It was arrived at through individual choices recognized in self and partner, and heightened because both parties are aware of what each created. This is improv support.

Listening to Your Partner.

Listen.

(To me now.)

Another one of the many things I've been told that is paramount to good improvisation is listening. Now surely I'm not going to refute that, am I?

"Listening to your partner on stage has got to be important in good improvisation—it just has to be."

Well it is, I guess, but in my opinion *merely* listening has little value. You have to know *how* to listen. Why do we listen? Is it to be polite?

When I was told to listen in an improv scene I just had to ask myself why. The answer seems obvious at first, but is it? Why is just listening important? I wasn't sure, but what I was sure about was merely being told to listen wasn't very helpful to me in improvisation. It was very passive and got me in my head. I certainly learned to shut up and listen to my partner, and I guess it was noble, but it rendered me passive and motionless on stage. It was another opportunity to think, to get in my head. Listening didn't help me at first.

After a while, after I learned for myself to create a character or point of view to arm myself in a scene, listening became a different thing.

I listened so that I could respond to operative information my partners supplied for me and filter it through my own character in the scene. I listened so it would help shape what I was going to do and say in the scene. Ah, it came back to *me* again. Listening gave me another tool, allowed me more ammunition to pour into what I had created.

Truly, merely listening is not enough. I listen to gain valuable opportunities to say or do something relevant through my character's voice, when I respond. That's why I listen.

Oh God, so selfish again. Isn't listening an altruistic act and can't it remain as such? Don't you listen because it's nice and it's give-and-take and give-and-take is good in improv and all of that?

Sure, but what does it leave me? Like it or not, improvisation is choices made by individuals, and individuals need to know what to do. Merely listening tells me nothing of what I have to do. Listening as a way to respond to given information through my character is a whole different thing.

What If I Am the Partner?

That is to say, what if I am the one not initiating, but responding in the scene?

I've talked a lot about just doing something at the top of the scene and making a strong initiation right off the top without thinking and catching up with it later. But what if someone beats me to it? Half the time that will happen. How do I respond and keep my own thing together in the scene?

Well, it's damn near the same thing as initiating the scene in the first place, with a couple more tools to boot.

If your partner initiates the scene, presumably with words, before you do, do this:

First of all, protect yourself in the scene even though you say no words. Even though you don't initiate, snap into a character or point of view or at least an emotional disposition at the very top, right when or slightly before the lights come up. Then you have your armor for the scene, even if your partner literally initiates the content with words. Now, when you respond to your partner, you already have something to respond through. Once again, not respond to, but respond *through*. And what that something is, is whatever you want it to be. If you do this, you've already won half the battle in responding in an improv scene: You've taken care of yourself first, regardless of whether you were the first to say something in the scene.

The other fifty percent of the battle in responding in an improv scene is what most people worry one hundred percent about:

"What words do I use when I respond in an improv scene?"

Simple but hard.

Use words that acknowledge your partner's initiation and adhere to your point of view or character.

Here's what that means.

Let's say your partner cheerfully initiates the line, "This letter is for you!" Let's also say that at the top of the scene you have snapped into a bored disposition. A response that would forward the scene might be an indifferent shrug and the words, "Put it on the table, I'll open it later." This response adheres to the point of view you've already created silently while also acknowledging your partner's initiation. It keeps you strong and allows you to now filter everything that happens in the scene through the space of "bored" or "indifferent." Another possible response, maintaining "bored," might be a tired, sarcastic, "Oh, let me open it, it's probably the sweepstakes," or "Great, more bills," or "Probably just another residual check."

I provide all of these examples to allow you to realize you have many options in acknowledgement of the reality of your partner's suggestion, and that once again, it's not as important *what* you say as long as you filter it through your point of view. With your words, you can agree to open the letter or not, who cares? As long as you acknowledge the reality of the letter, and the words come from the bored space you created at the top of the scene, the rest doesn't really matter.

Some might say that to *not* open the letter is to reject your partner's suggestion or that it's blocking the scene. I say no. It depends on what the character would do. Some characters wouldn't open the letter. Others would. In some cases, heightening of character and thereby heightening of relationship is achieved to a greater degree by a character's decision not to do something as opposed to doing it.

This may be difficult to grasp because of the concept of *yes*: "Say yes to everything." I say that's fine if you want to live in the magical fantasy land of "Improv is a love-fest and everything is as good as pie." But a good, a good, a good improviser will let the character do the talking, even if the talking happens to be about the refusal to act on something.

The most important thing, in my opinion, in responding in an improv scene is to respond out of your character's voice and acknowledge your partner's initiation as reality: agreeing with the circumstances your partner declares, but not feeling like you have to say yessy yes to everything they say.

What happens if you find yourself without a character at the top of the scene?

If you find that when the lights come up, you have not made a choice of what your particular deal is before your partner initiates, get something quick.

I mean quick.

Otherwise, you risk getting into a measured state and finding yourself in your head. Say something and snap into something. I'm not talking frenetic, I'm just saying you have a greater chance of finding power for yourself if you respond quickly, any way you can.

Improvisers who have made a strong character choice at the top of a scene can really take their time before responding. For example, the same bored character from above, getting the initiation "This letter's for you," could slowly turn, gaze, roll his eyes, look away, look back, sigh, and slowly say, "Great, another letter from my dear mother." His response is not fear-and-confusion-filled silence, it's offering the *choice* of silence before responding.

Unfortunately, most silence before a response is not choice in improvisation. It's someone that has no game and they are silent out of fear and not power. So if you find yourself in that space, I suggest responding quickly with something just to snap you out of your head a bit. You may do okay with no initial choice and four seconds of silence before you talk, but in my book you increase your chances of a good scene if you respond and acknowledge quickly.

I'm often asked in class, "What if both my partner and I have initiated at the same time—who responds?" If you are in the rare scene where that occurs, follow through with what you have created, hold on to it, and then respond. It is even more rare that both of you would *respond* at the same moment. If you were unable to hear your partner's initiation because you were both speaking at the same time, restate what you initiated.

Here's another little trick in responding to an initiation in an improv scene. Take on the other person's character. Respond as the character or point of view that they have created.

What? Sounds like cheating.

No, not at all.

Let's say your partner initiates a scene slumped over and in a gravelly voice holds out his hand and says, "Got a quarter?" Obviously, a homeless person wanting money. Ninety percent of improvisers would take on the persona of a businessperson passing by and go with the obvious choice of being indignant and say, "Get a job" or whatever. Imagine another choice: In the same voice and same posture you immediately respond with "No, do you?" Now you have a scene between two homeless people. You are already in an aligned space.

Another example: In a British accent your partner initiates, "Nice day, don't you think?" Without a blink, you respond, also in a high-status British dialect, "So lovely. Tea?" Now you have a scene with two British people. The audience is not thinking, "That guy stole the other guy's character." No, they are thinking, "Oh, a scene between two British people." It's a great way to immediately acknowledge your partner's suggestion and forward the scene. Your partner doesn't mind, either. It's affirming to have someone take on your energy and it feels good to immediately snap into the same agreed-upon space of being. You don't want to do that every time you do a scene, but it's a great thing when the right context (which you'll know when you see it) comes up. Taking on your partner's character could also include his wants and needs, movement, and rhythms.

My idea of supporting your partner in improvisation is not waiting, but choosing and doing. Maintain and heighten your choice and you will support your partner in the beginning, in the middle, and throughout the scene.

Context and Scenes

So let's assume you succeeded in creating a strong space for yourself at the top of the scene and so has your partner.

The beginning of the scene was met with play and now you have two points of view or characters on stage even if they're the same or not. You have the makings of a good scene.

Now what?

I believe I've already mentioned that you'll want to hold on to whatever it is that you've created, for sure. Now you just have to play it for all it's worth. You have all the tools before you, to up your chances.

What does *playing* it mean? It means making more of that which you have already created. It means *realizing the context* that has been created, playing *within* that context, and all the while making *surprising* choices.

Context is everything. Not just in improvisation, but in everything. Let's take a big look at context.

Context

Context is everything in everything.

What the—?

It is the frame for all great works and the unspoken credo of everyday living. Let me explain. Human beings cannot function unless they are provided context for living. Human beings cannot observe unless provided context. Human beings cannot enjoy unless provided context. All of life has many contexts. All good movies, books, plays, or songs have context. All good improvisation has context. An agreed-upon road map for living. Context affects all things.

Am I big on context?

You bet.

Context allows a human being to know what to expect. It is necessary in life and in a scene. In life, surprises within a context become theatrical; in improvisation, surprises within a context usually result in laughter. Let's talk about contexts in life, first.

A school is an institution for learning. Children go there daily. There are teachers and books and chalkboards and chairs and we all know that. We all know what to expect from the context of school. Add a clown. A clown comes to school. It is still school, but it is a special day where a clown is coming to a classroom to entertain the kids. It is still *within the context of school:* a bit surprising and theatrical but still, a mostly *unsurprising* school event. Add a gun, instead. A kid bringing a gun to school and shooting classmates is tragic and surprising within the context of school, and is nationwide news, thus theatrical. Add a lot of guns. After years of school shootings the overall context of *what could happen at school* broadens to include the possibility of kids getting shot; the event of a school shooting diminishes. The tenth school shooting gets less coverage than the first. You might even hear someone say, after learning of the second school shooting in a week, "That's horrible, but I'm not surprised." What they are saying is, "My context for what it means to go to school has come to include the everyday possibility of a shooting. Therefore, while still tragic, it is not as much of an event, so it does not really surprise me."

Here is an example of how context can change:

1. A businessman is walking down a city street in a tan overcoat and carrying a briefcase. Normal within a city street context, not very eventful. Nobody pays attention to him and there are a thousand others just like him.

2. A businessman in the same attire is, instead, jogging down the city street. Not as common, but not an event either. Not an event because we assume his *context* for him. He's probably late or running for a cab or bus. Normal, given that context. The businessman himself adheres to the context with a kind of jog, as opposed to a full-out sprint, because he knows the sprint will take him into the embarrassing realm of inappropriate business behavior in a city. He will adhere to that appropriate context no matter how late he is.

3. A businessman is sprinting pretty fast, each time hiking his knees well above his waistline, and trotting in a straight line. He becomes theater. He looks silly, given the context of appropriate behavior for a businessman on a city street. People look at him and snicker. He is behaving out of context.

4. The same businessman, in the same exact action, is in the musical *How to Succeed in Business Without Really Trying*. Theatrical because it is a musical, but certainly not an inappropriate social context because he is acting within the confines of being in a musical theatre production.

5. Take any of the above scenarios (except the musical) and add that it is 100° outside. The businessman would seem inappropriate in this context because he is wearing a coat. He might get a couple of glances.

Here's another example: A man in sweatpants and sweatshirt is standing by the corner of a building and screaming at the top of his lungs. You are about to come upon him and walk off the sidewalk into the street to avoid him. You are slightly scared because you assess him as a crazy street person. As you walk into the street you see a woman in sweat pants and sweatshirt just around the corner. She was previously hidden by part of the building but now she is exposed as you enter the street. The woman is crying and angry. Ah-ha, not a crazy guy. It's a guy yelling at his wife or girlfriend and they are wearing sweat pants because they were both out on a jog. The context shifts, and so do you. Take the same guy screaming, take away the woman, and put the guy on stage. Now you have a ranting monologue. Context truly is everything. Context truly changes everything.

"What are people wearing to the party?" is an attempt to adhere to an appropriate social context. You don't want to look "out of place." "Should we bring a bottle of wine to the dinner?" is not so much asking out of your intense desire to bring a bottle of wine, as it is to be socially appropriate in the dinner invitation context.

In the office context, you wear office attire, except perhaps on Friday. In the Friday context, you dress a bit more casually. Not too wild, but more casual. At the office Halloween party, you'd better dress in a costume. In that context, formal or casual business attire would be inappropriate; a costume is necessary. Not dressing that way would be socially incorrect, given the context of the event.

Humans assess contexts all day long without even thinking about it and act accordingly. Context is their road map for living.

People themselves have contexts also, day to day, and in life in general. "He's a whiner" or "She's always got something nice to say" are contexts humans assign themselves or others.

If the nicest guy at work is suddenly a jerk, we say, "He's not himself today." He's acting out of sorts; he's behaving outside of his general life context. Even day to day, if you are asked, "How are you?" and you respond with, "I'm tired and I feel a little sick," you declare the context for yourself that day. You will fulfill that context all day long, having everything you say and do adhere to it. You will make sure that your road map for the day is adhered to in every way. Even if you feel not sick and wide awake one hour after your declaration, quite often you will fake it just to remain within your predefined "I don't feel well today" context. You will act sick and tired all day just to be true to how you said you felt.

Now let's bring context to the realm of entertainment. Using my standby *Wizard of Oz* example, what are some of its contexts? One is its color. In Kansas, we see black and white film, in Oz, color. That's a context declaration for the movie that must never be violated, and it isn't. Another context is the yellow brick road. It's a literal contextual road map for the characters and the audience. We expect them to stay on it, and when they don't there's trouble. A third is desire. Dorothy desires to go home. She meets the Scarecrow, who desires a brain, and the Tin Man, who desires a heart. After that contextual declaration, it would indeed be tragic if when Dorothy meets the Lion, the Lion is complacent and desires nothing. But we are not disappointed, for indeed, just as the film declared, the Lion desires courage. A final great overall context for *The Wizard of Oz* is that it was all a dream. A retroactive announcement at the end of the movie informs the audience that all they have seen is Dorothy's dream. Nothing violated the dream aspect in Oz, and the color context even enhanced the dreamlike quality.

Scenes

Okay, great.

And please God what does this have to do with improvising scenes?

Well, let's go to scenes in improv games, first. A game many know is Freeze Tag, or Switch, as some call it. If you don't know it, it's a staple improv game where two people step forward from the group and start a scene. A player from the group yells, "Freeze!" The two people in the scene freeze in position, and the player who yelled "Freeze!" tags one of the frozen players out, takes their *exact* physical position, and initiates a whole new scene with a different location and characters, justifying the frozen physical positions. The first scene of Freeze Tag usually begins with the suggestion of a line of dialogue provided by the audience.

So what is the context of Freeze Tag? It's "how the game is played," as explained in the previous paragraph. The audience is informed how the game works in an introduction. Now they know the context, the road map, what they are supposed to enjoy.

We first say something like, "We're going to improvise a game for you now." Why announce that first? You want to let the audience know that you are in the realm, the context of, making it up versus performing something that you wrote and rehearsed. That context lets the audience know you may be improvisationally unfinished and reckless. Then you explain the game. After the audience knows the context of the game—how to play it—you get a line from them to start the scene. Using their suggestion ensures the context of improvisation. While playing Freeze Tag, a player doesn't yell "Freeze!" and then continue the previous scene or yell "Freeze!" and pop in, ignore the previous scene's physical position, and begin another scene. That would be in violation of the declared context. (When players do make these moves in Freeze Tag, the audience may react negatively or seem confused because of the violation, as may the other players on stage).

Think of any game you can and you will find that it has a context, and that its context is usually announced before the game begins.

Improvisation itself has contexts. In long-form improvisation you take a single suggestion and improvise for about half an hour. We don't violate that by taking a suggestion and improvising for two minutes and then taking another suggestion. Within long-form improvisation there are other structured contexts. We call them *new forms*. Time is a context to describe the *art form* of improvisation. There is *short form* and *long form*. (Bizarrely, it's the only *art form* which categorizes itself in length of time.)

Let's journey on into the purely improvised scene.

Do purely improvised scenes have contexts? Yes, yes. Every single one of them.

Here's a sample improv scene I just made up. It is a man and a woman with the following dialogue:

MAN: I can't wait to go to the birthday party.

WOMAN: Yeah, Jimmy is really gonna be surprised.

MAN: Everyone's gonna be there.

WOMAN: I got him a gift certificate from the Gap.

MAN: That's great. He really deserves a party after all his hard work.

WOMAN: I couldn't agree more.

What is the context of this stupid little scene?

At this point, one might say that the context is *talking about going to a party*.

If I were in this improv scene, I would stay in the realm of *talking about things that were about the party*. If I violate that, I violate the scene.

Hmmm. So is the context of a scene merely *what people are talking about*?

Some people think so. Some people think that what improvisers are talking about is what the scene is about and what the entire context is. But wait, I forgot about the how of the scene. I forgot to mention that both of them are saying their lines extremely sarcastically and laugh every once in awhile.

MAN: (raising an eyebrow) I can't wait to go to the birthday party.

WOMAN: (snickering) Yeah, Jimmy is really gonna be surprised.

MAN: (indicating around him) Everyone's gonna be there.

WOMAN: (laughing) I got him a gift certificate from the Gap.

MAN: (sarcastic) That's great. He really deserves a party after all his haaaard wooork.

WOMAN: (sighing/raising eyebrow) I couldn't agree more.

With this information, the context of the scene shifts entirely. *How you do something* in an improv scene is vital to establishing its context. The context is no longer the literal meaning of the words being said, nor is that what the scene is about. It is about sarcasm. Given this context, the scene opens up. It allows for other things to be talked about, as long as they remain in the land of sarcasm. The next line could be:

MAN: (sneering) Speaking of parties, working with you is a party every day.

WOMAN: (smirking) Yeah. Oh, that must be why you always show up so fashionably late.

The sarcasm is the context, plain and simple. The words can open up, as long as they carry the declared cadence of sarcasm. In this scene, you declare to the audience that the road map for the scene is that all things will be sarcastic.

Oh, I forgot to mention that during this scene, both the man and the woman are in the middle of performing surgery in an operating room. And they are doing it without really looking at the patient while randomly throwing his organs on the floor. Now with the words themselves, how they are said, and the scene's physical activity, the context becomes: *being snitty and gossipy is more important than high-stakes operation.* This new context opens the scene up even more.

So if I'm the guy in the scene above, what do I do next? What do I play?

Once I know the context of the scene, I'm golden. *Things that are about being gossipy while performing my job with indifference.* Infinite possibilities: new people to talk about, another patient, not scrubbing before the next surgery, hosing down the operating table for the next patient while talking about so-and-so's kids, etc. As long as I stay in that context, I'm fine. The audience knows the road map of the scene—its context—and is only thinking, "Do more of that bad surgery sarcastic thing."

As I said at the beginning of this chapter, though, it's not good enough for an improviser to merely remain within and maintain a context. No, you must declare the context for the audience, and then surprise from within that context. Let's go back to *The Wizard of Oz* (I'm so sorry).

It is not sufficient to land Dorothy in Oz and then spend two hours merely showing different shots of her traversing a brick road alone with Toto. Even if you were to add shots of Oz becoming closer and closer, it would be boring and uneventful. The context remains the same (Dorothy's desire to go home and travelling the yellow road to get there), but to maintain it is just plain dull. It's *merely* maintaining its context. So what does *The Wizard of Oz* do? Surprises from within the context: witches, flying monkeys, and poppy fields. Dorothy's great, but she doesn't hold up by herself for long. She has to meet a Scarecrow, a Tin Man, and a frightened Lion. And these three don't all want a brain, no, only one of them. They must all want something, but it would be less interesting in this particular context for them to all want the same thing. Surprise from within: The trees talk and they are throwing apples at us. Never violate the context but *do* surprise us.

In improvisation, those surprises usually result in your audience's laughter. Once the audience understands your road map for the scene, make choices that surprise them.

In the sample improv scene, if the man and woman *merely* sarcastically repeated over and over again that they were going to the party while performing surgery, the scene may or may not hold up. There's a better chance, though, that it will run out of steam. So how do you surprise? You talk about other things and perform other physical activities inappropriate to an operating room. You build *sarcastic* to *condescending* and to *just plain hateful*. You open up the scene this way; you broaden the elements of the mutually declared context. Create your own flying monkeys. Surprise the audience with your choices.

Abbott and Costello can't use the *same* mistaken pronoun for every baseball player in "Who's on First"—they must open it up to other names and other mistaken identities.

Even in an improv game, where the context is predefined and announced, we rely on the intelligence of the players to surprise the audience and each other with their choices.

In improvisation, maintaining is not good enough for an effective scene; improvisers must constantly bring new elements to the context they have created.

Another scene example: Let's say the lights come up on Tom and Bill.

TOM: (clearly paranoid) I-I-I think we sh-sh-should get outta h-here.

Get out of where? *Who cares*—it's the first line. It's more important *that* he says something and *how* he said it: *paranoid* and *stuttery*. That demeanor becomes his context for that moment. He must own it.

BILL: (in a strong, gruff voice) Nonsense, just reach your hand out.

Where are they? *Who cares*—it's the second line. More important that the second guy has taken care of himself with the point of view of *strong* and *confident*. Reach his hand out where? *Who cares?* It's how he plays it that will get him through the scene. What's their relationship? Oh, it's a paranoid guy and a confident guy together. The label of their relationship is unimportant now; it will probably show up in a much more deft fashion later than if forced by one of them at the top of the scene. Relax.

TOM: (still paranoid, but reaching out) I-I'm af-f-fraid.

Golden. *What?* Golden because he retained his point of view and stuttered. He told the audience, his partner, and himself that when he said the first line, in the way he said it, he literally *knew what he was doing*. He proved it when he did it the second time. When you do something twice in improvisation, you establish a pattern.

BILL: Books don't bite, kid. It's not a gator!

This guy established a pattern, too. A pattern of mentoring and confidence. These two are right on track.

TOM: B-But there's people ar-r-round.
BILL: Of course there's people in a library, now grab the damn book!

(Tom is doing fine; his words are filtered through the paranoia and stuttering. Bill decides to clarify the location. Fine, but what's more important is that he continues to play his gruff confidence. We really know he's okay in the scene when he demands, "Now grab the damn book!" because he restores his earlier demand in the scene.

TOM: B-But D-Dad, I . . .
BILL: No son of mine is going to be scared of a little learning, now pick it up!

Tom establishes himself as the son, broadening the context to include the label of the relationship. Now he can filter being in a father/son relationship through the more important overall context, his paranoia and fear. Bill played a great response. He used Tom's label of Father/Son to interrupt Tom (which is what Bill's character would do) and further demand something of him with stern confidence. The context of this scene is intact and it has broadened. It's not about the literal words anymore. These characters can say *nearly* anything as long as they retain their respective dispositions.

TOM: (hesitantly picks a book and looks at the title)"H-How to C-C-C-Command Author-r-r-ity."
BILL: (screaming quickly) *Read it now!*

Still on track, these two. Tom knows that in improv, even if you have a negative disposition about something, it's probably better to do the thing asked of you and *keep* your negative opinion about doing it. It just propels the scene. (An exception to this would be a character whose declared context at the top of the scene is that he will not do things.) Tom's choice for title of the book was not a random reference. It was entirely in line with his paranoid context. A good choice, the title suggests the exact opposite of his capabilities. The title was surprising from within the context of the scene. Bill surprised us with his extreme volume and abruptness. We knew him to be confident and gruff, but he startled us with just how much he was so.

So at this point in this scene, what are these two improvisers thinking? I would imagine that they are, in a sort of nonconscious way, thinking:

TOM: I must demonstrate more ways to be paranoid and stutter.

BILL: I must be more demanding, confident, and gruff.

Things that are about the point of view. Surprising things. Yes.

Since the context of the scene is set, they are probably thinking these thoughts in a sort of super-alert conscious/not-conscious/subconscious way.

Tom and Bill are in the middle of a decent scene, with a lot of room for growth. If two improvisers are in that kind of scene, here's what they are probably *not* thinking:

- "I'd better not ask a question."
- "What's my *who, what, where.*"
- "I'd better not talk about the past."
- "I'd better not say *no.*"
- "I'd better not create conflict."
- "I'd better create conflict.

You get my hateful point. Good improvisation isn't thinking about those things. It's finding your individual deal with another's individual deal and realizing a common context and surprising from within it. Plain and simple.

6 Common Problems

Over the years, I've noticed common things improvisers do when they give up power in an improv scene. Improvisers are (more or less) human beings and human beings have behavioral patterns. Sometimes these patterns help in improvisation; sometimes they do not. I would like to discuss a few and you may decide whether they apply to you.

These are *not* rules.

These are individual problems that sometimes show up in individual improvisers. Some of them may apply to you and some of them may not. If they apply to you, great. If they don't, think no more about them and have a good time improvising.

Too Much Exposition

At the top of the scene, an improviser spills the beans with a big line of exposition: "I'm glad you, my brother, are here because we must wash the car before mother and father arrive at the apartment here at noon to discuss my getting fired from my factory job."

Some improvisers love to provide bulky exposition at the top of a scene. They think they need the safety of that construct to improvise the scene. A lot of this comes from being told at some point to "establish the *who*, *what,* and *where* in the first three lines of the scene." Nowadays, that fashion of exposition reads really stale to an audience and puts an unneeded burden on the scene. The audience knows that people don't talk like that, and it is disconcerting to them.

If it is absolutely important to you to have exposition at the top of an improv scene, dole it out gracefully, a little at a time. If, however, you make attacking the scene with a powerful declaration more important, you will find that the exposition you do provide will be backed up with a more substantial point of view and will be more deftly placed in the scene. It will be coming from a more powerful and organic place.

Talking Too Much

This is a problem I have, so I'm very aware of it. It's the "I will keep talking until I find something that works" thing. It's easy to fix once you're aware of it.

Quite often improvisers with this problem subconsciously use the words "I mean" to allow themselves to keep talking.

> IMPROVISER: I just don't think you should visit your brother, I mean, every time you visit him something bad happens, I mean, you remember the last time you visited him, I mean, when he started calling you names, I mean, I think you should just stay home.

When the words "I mean" show up often, it usually means that improvisers are searching for what they mean. They keep talking until they find it.

Here's how to find out if you talk too much when you improvise.

Make a conscious choice, in a class or on stage, to say one short sentence at a time. Choose that context for yourself ahead of time. If, when you are improvising in that context, you have a need to talk more, or if you feel stifled by just saying a short sentence, there's a good chance that you've unconsciously conditioned yourself to talk more than you need to.

If you discover that you are one of these improvisers, practice improvising one sentence and not speaking until your partner responds. Put a period after your sentences and then shut the hell up. You will solve your problem quickly if you do this a few times. Then you will notice that when you do talk more, it is because of a choice and not a consequence of having conditioned yourself to keep talking.

It is interesting that people don't really know they are talking too much. They're too busy talking to realize how much they are talking. Ah, that I could give the gift of potential energy to improvisers who have multitudes of kinetic energy.

Imagine the above example this way:

I just don't think you should visit your brother.

Hold.

Hold.

Hold.

Feel the power.

Hold.

Wait.

Strong.

Hold.

Potential energy. Don't let the air out of creation by talking so much.

Justifying

Justifying goes hand in hand with the above two examples. Beginning improvisers do it all the time. What is it? It is when you make an initiation and then justify *why* you said or did that initiation. You do or say something and then soon after explain why you did that. It's tricky and subjective.

A blatant example of justifying:

Cop A: That street lamp is out.
Cop B: Yeah, whatever.

Cop A: Well, it's really dark.

Cop B: So what?

Cop A: It's just weird, I mean, every time we walk the beat together you act indifferent to me. I . . .

The last line is the justification, and like everything, whether or not it's a problem depends on how it's said and when it is said. I would imagine in this example, the justification is a consequence of fear on the part of the improviser playing Cop A. In this case, he wigged out at the indifference of the second improviser's character and resorted to making an assessment of the scene. First with, "It's just weird," meaning, "I as the improviser am confused so I will assess that the situation is *weird* because it's the only way I can protect myself."

Then comes the "I mean," which we've already discussed.

Then comes the justification, "Every time we walk the beat together you act indifferent to me." This is an attempt to explain *why* Cop B is behaving the way she is. It is too scary for some improvisers to just allow the other improviser to *be* in the scene, so they have to justify a situation or assess someone's behavior.

The "I . . ." is there because quite often, after a justification such as this, the improviser will continue talking.

I placed the justification in this scene where it is on purpose. That is, quite often, justifications come after the second or third exchange in the scene. That's where a weaker improviser will become uncomfortable with the scene and want to dilute the mystery by answering the question, "Why are we behaving like this?" It is very much out of fear; an adult, left-brain need to apply logic and answers to the mystery of the behavior of the scene.

Almost always the improviser feels a little icky after such moments and the audience feels the power loss, but neither the performer nor the audience knows why. The reason that it causes a drop in the scene is because the play of the scene is explained and not allowed to just be. It would be like either Abbott or Costello turning to the audience and saying, "In case you didn't realize it, we are using pronouns in the place of baseball players' names." That would be a drag because it explains why the behavior is happening, as opposed to letting us enjoy that it is happening. We want to enjoy the confusion in "Who's on First," not have it explained to us.

In my example, it would be different if the *first* sentence of the scene were, "Every time we walk the beat you seem indifferent to me." It would be different because out of the gate, the declared behavior would be accusatory, which could be played like anything else. It becomes a justification if it is presented later in the scene to explain why previous behavior in the scene has been exhibited.

Another very common example of justification in improvisation is the calling-someone-crazy thing. It happens in a scene where someone is exhibiting behavior that the other person can't figure out. The scene goes on for a bit (probably unfunnily), and the confused improviser blurts out something like, "Well, you're just crazy."

Ultimate justification.

I don't understand your improvisation behavior (and I probably haven't created any powerful choice for myself either), therefore I am going to accuse you of being crazy. I'm going to justify your behavior, explain why you are behaving that way. You must be crazy. It happens a lot.

It's ironic because in improvisation we hope for crazy. We want elevated theatrical absurd behavior; we just don't want it called out.

It's sometimes difficult to determine whether you justify when you improvise, but here is a clue to help you out.

If you are improvising, and around the third beat you notice that you say a long sentence and then feel a little weird, there's a good chance that was the justification. If it then feels kinda fake to get back into the scene, there's a greater chance it was one. (Imagine trying to resume "Who's on First?" after having called out that someone is mistaking baseball players' names for pronouns.)

If you've noticed that you do that, you've achieved the first step in rectifying justifying. Now, the next time you improvise you will know it's likely that a justification might come up in the second or third exchange. When you feel it coming (don't worry, you will feel it) do anything but blurt that line out. I rarely tell someone not to do something, but it's about the only way to get through this improvisational block. Instead of saying that line, hold it back in silence, even if it takes four seconds of near stuttering. Then think of your last line, the last line you said, and restate. Say it again in a slightly different way. This trick will train you not only to not justify, but also to hold on to the power of your first declaration, your point of view. So, in the cop example:

COP A: That street lamp is out.
COP B: Yeah, whatever.
COP A: Well, it's really dark.
COP B: So what?
(Pause. Hang on.)
COP A: It's so dark, I can't even see.

The first time you do this you will feel the value, and justification will leave your improvisation soon after.

There are a slew of words and phrases in justification land that I have noticed throughout the years. In many of the following cases, if the lines were said with any strong deal behind them, they would be perfectly fine. I have noticed, however, that ninety-nine percent of the time, they are said with nothing behind them and in a kind of pleading, weak cadence.

Here are some of the more common examples.

First Day

This is my first day of being a mechanic, what do you do?

First day at the bank, first day at the racetrack, first day of college, all explain *why* the behavior that follows will be incompetent and uninformed. It's an apology even before the scene starts.

First Time

This is my first time in a hot air balloon

Same as *first day*, *first time* describes why I will be confused or incompetent.

Every Time We/You

Every time we come to the park, you fight with me.

Usually offered as the second or third exchange in a scene.

I Love/I Hate

I love working in a factory.

or

I hate ice cream.

This line is usually spoken right out of the gate, after a moment of confused silence, and is a desperate attempt to justify a suggestion by an audience. It also often sounds sophomoric, almost child or caveman-like.

This Is The Best ___ Ever

This is the best Groundhog Day ever.

Usually spoken in the middle of a troubled scene and used in order to justify half-hearted good-feeling prior behavior.

___Is Fun

Flying kites is fun.

Things that are confusing to improvisers often become "fun" for them.

It is almost a plea for the audience to have fun while they are watching the improviser not have fun saying something is fun.

Listen.

"Raking leaves is fun!" (Said with no character and little emotion other than the improviser's desperate attempt to act like he/she is having fun.)

"Working in a factory is fun!" (Said after a long silence that follows the suggestion of "Factory!" as a location.)

"Flying kites is fun!"

No. It really isn't.

What I'm hoping you *don't* read into my spewing about justification is that you'd better not say the words and phrases I've listed above. What I *do* hope you get is that these words and phrases are my observations of the patterns created through justifying in improvisation. By being on the lookout for them when you improvise or observe improvisation, you will learn to avoid them.

Pausing

Two improvisers who haven't taken care of themselves at the top of the scene will often get into a measured, "pause before you say a line" kind of scene with the following pace:

> IMPROVISER A: What's up? (pause, pause, pause, pause, two, three, four)
>
> IMPROVISER B: Not much. (Pause, pause, pause, pause, two, three, four)
>
> IMPROVISER A: So . . . (Pause, pause, pause, pause, two, three, four)

This goes on forever. The funny (but unfortunately not) thing about it is that most of the time the improvisers are not even aware of the tremendous silence between their lines. That's because they are *thinking* so hard.

So hard.

Thinking about what to do and say and what not to say and do and—you know.

If you find yourself in this mode, or are fortunate enough to have someone tell you, or if you just notice that your scenes are unfunny and drag on a lot, then do this:

Make a game out of not letting yourself have any pauses when you improvise.

Know, going into class or rehearsal or a show, that in your scene you will make a game out of responding *immediately* after your partner has said a line. This game will throw you out of your head in a good way and remind you that it is more important *that* you say something now than *what* you say.

Remember that the good scenes you have done, the scenes that were magical, probably didn't have a pause quality going on; rather, they had a feeling of rapid fire, even if they were slow scenes.

"Is this to say that I should never have pauses between any of my lines, then?"

No, again. If a powerful improviser makes a choice of pausing before lines at the top or very near the top of a scene, then that becomes that improviser's deal and it's fine. It's pauses as a consequence of fear, when an improviser is thinking, that this condition applies to.

Bailing on a Point of View

It's so tempting and so easy to shift your point of view in an improv scene, and ninety-nine percent of the time it pulls the rug out from underneath the scene.

It takes a while for improvisers to learn that they can go longer with a point of view, character, emotional state, and so on than they think they can. Improvisers make a choice at the top of a scene and then judge their own creation and attempt to change their mind. If they don't get laughs right away or other affirmation from their audience, they are sometimes quick to throw their whole bloody idea away.

There is a particular moment in improvisation, a threshold improvisers reach, when they must decide to pursue or abandon an idea they have created. Experienced improvisers have learned not to freak out when that uncomfortable threshold arises, but to take a breath and persevere.

Penetrating through those fear thresholds and sustaining your creation will reap you greater benefits on the other side. It takes guts and experience to hold on to your own vision, on stage and off. We're so conditioned to change our minds if something doesn't work out immediately that we bring this behavior on stage. In our contract with the audience to make more of the truth we have created, we must sustain our visions and creations regardless of how afraid we feel in the moment.

A tidy way to practice holding on when you feel like shifting is to restate your claim. I'll explain.

IMPROVISER A: I don't feel well.

IMPROVISER B: Well, you're going to school anyway.

IMPROVISER A: Yeah, but I don't feel well.

IMPROVISER B: Get your coat on.

It's at this point in the scene where Improviser A has to decide whether to hang on or shift. The "I don't feel well" thing isn't cutting it. A lot of improvisers might give in and respond:

IMPROVISER B: Get your coat on.

IMPROVISER A: Okay. I have a math test.

Or whatever. It's the "Okay" that signals you've changed your mind in the scene and dilutes that which you have already created. In those moments you want to restate your position and up the ante:

IMPROVISER B: Get your coat on.

IMPROVISER A: I think I'm dying. Yes, I'm definitely going to die.

You can go to school or not but you must hit that beat hard with your point of view and persevere. If you feel like bailing in an improv scene hit it even harder, instead. After a while, those moments won't be as scary and it will become second nature for you to get through that fear threshold.

Some might say that by holding on to "sick," Improviser A is blocking and resisting the course of the scene. I say, *not if that's what the scene is about from the get-go.* It would be a far greater violation to shift what has already been declared as true: that Improviser A doesn't feel well.

The above are some common issues I've noticed improvisers share. If you can first identify them and then go through some growing pains making alterations, you will end up on the other side a stronger, more powerful (and funnier) performer.

◤ More Than Two People in a Scene

Three-Person Scenes

A scene with three people is its own animal. It requires a bit of finesse and timing that a two-person scene doesn't. The biggest reason people screw up a three-person scene is that they think "different" when they could have thought "same." Here's what I mean: The lights come up and you discover there are suddenly three people on stage. Let's say the scene goes down like this:

IMPROVISER A: It's such a beautiful Sunday!

IMPROVISER B: I've got the picnic basket ready!

IMPROVISER C: (says nothing)

IMPROVISER A: I'm glad the kids are with Grandma.

IMPROVISER B: I've got tuna, lemonade, and apple pie!

IMPROVISER C: (says nothing, continues to wonder about his function in the scene.)

IMPROVISER A: Let's go have a picnic!

IMPROVISER C: Wait, I don't think we should go right now, I'm not feeling well.

This is a fairly typical beginning of a three-person scene. Two people get on track with something. The third person just stands there silently trying to figure out what to do, while the other two continue. Aware that if his silence persists, it soon won't seem right to speak at all, Improviser C blurts out something adverse to or different from what Improvisers A and B have initiated. This is what I mean by *thinking different*.

It's very tempting for the third person to take a contrary point of view. He may do so because he thinks he needs to create conflict and subconsciously believes that being different will give him power in the scene. Go with the flow, especially in a group scene. You don't have time to work around a lot of tangential points of view. This advice also holds true for a scene that starts out with two negative but similar points of view:

IMPROVISER A: I hate the way that dress looks on her.

IMPROVISER B: Yeah, I hope she didn't get gypped at the Salvation Army.

IMPROVISER C: I kinda like it.

Another example of a disrupted initiation. Improviser C would have gained a lot more ground with:

IMPROVISER C: Picture perfect white trash.

Go with. The audience is trying to cipher out what the scene is about. They like seeing "Those people talk about the way that person's dressed." Simple. That's what the scene is about.

It's as likely, though, that in a three-person scene the first two initiators won't even share a common point of view among themselves at the top of the scene:

IMPROVISER A: This coffee is delicious.

IMPROVISER B: Really? I think it tastes terrible.

Now what is the third improviser to do? I say take one of the existing positions. In the banal scene above, declare that your coffee is either delicious or terrible, thereby joining an existing point of view, or make up a different taste reaction to the coffee, joining the point of view *that coffee is being tasted*:

IMPROVISER A: This coffee is delicious.
IMPROVISER B: Really? I think it tastes terrible.
IMPROVISER C: Mine tastes kinda bitter, but I like it.

Improviser C made a move to heighten the notion of reacting to coffee, as opposed to:

IMPROVISER A: This coffee is delicious.
IMPROVISER B: Really? I think it tastes terrible.
IMPROVISER C: Who cares? Let's play baseball.

In the last example, Improviser C comes in with something different and now the scene kinda has to start over with finding what it is about. A similar point of view does not have to be expressed only by words; it could be done through character, emotion, or state of mind, as well. An example of this might be

IMPROVISER A (angrily): The sky is blue!
IMPROVISER B (angrily): I like Cheerios!
IMPROVISER C (angrily): Birds fly!

That all of them are angry declares their shared point of view, even if they are saying different things. The audience identifies that the scene is about *three angry people*. Also, the content is all unrelated non sequiturs, therefore declaring *nonsense* as a shared point of view.
Huh?
Yes.
Think same, not different, in three-person scenes. Especially with character. I've seen the following scene 8,452 times (more or less):

IMPROVISER A (in French accent): The water is so lovely.
IMPROVISER B (in French accent): The park is so nice this time
    of year.

IMPROVISER C (in American accent): Can you tell me how to get to . . .?

Oh, if Improviser C had just taken on a French accent he would have gained a lot more ground. As an American character, his choice makes the *circumstance of the scene*—finding directions and his American accent—more important than what the scene is already about: two French people enjoying their surroundings. He could have joined in a delightful scene between three French people, free to continue in the established scene that is *about French people*. *Being French* is their collective point of view: They can now talk about *anything* as those French people. Instead, he made an opposite (and often done) choice of being different, and the scene is forced to shift in order to deal with the *circumstance* he has brought forth. It's not just French people, either. The same would hold true if it were two robots, two sad people, two wiggly people, whatever.

Entering Scenes

The same principles apply to entering a two-person scene and becoming the third party. Before we speak of *how* to enter a scene, let's look at *why* people enter two-person scenes. Here, for the good or bad, are some reasons people enter scenes:

■ Save it.
You're backstage during a scene and it starts to drag or go a little long. You start thinking, "How can I save this scene?" Suddenly, you start thinking about lines and physical things and characters you will enter with in order to save it.

■ Get in on the funny.
"That scene is so funny, I'm gonna enter it and get in on all that hot action."

■ End it.
You're backstage and think that it's time for the scene to end, so you think of a reason to enter and "hook" the scene.

- Get a quick laugh.
"I'll just dart in and off stage or walk across and get a quick laugh."

- Tag out.
You get an idea and decide you want to tag out a player and take his place with another character. The player not tagged out usually maintains her character from the previous scene.

- Get called onstage.
You hear, "Uncle Jim should be coming over any second now," and you enter as Uncle Jim.

Knowing why you are entering is the first thing to consider.

Saving a scene in trouble is no easy task. Most of the time, the players are already in a state of measurement (in their head), and the audience is aware that the scene is going downhill. While you might have good intentions, your entrance may also just make things worse.

As soon as you enter, the audience is on to you. They usually have a sense that you have entered to bring the scene back to life. They are often thinking, "Damn, I thought it was going to be over soon." So you've got that going against you.

In addition, the person entering often takes a contrary or different point of view from what already exists on stage. This prolongs conflict and delays resolution, thereby lengthening the scene even more.

If, however, you provide a lightning-quick resolution or something different enough, you may be able to manufacture enough of a reason for the lights to be taken out. In this case, you're not helping or saving a scene, you're eliminating it, which we'll touch on in a bit.

About the only way to save a scene and allow it to continue is this:

Identify an existing energy, style, point of view, emotion, and so on, and take it on as you enter, just as you would when navigating a three-person scene.

You may be tempted to enter with something very different because the existing point of view is not working. I still say, "Think same, not different." A scene that isn't working needs validation and heightening, not apology and a declaration that what's happened up to this moment is bad. The entrance with a new or different point of view tells the audience, "I know it's bad, see, that's why I'm trying to change it by doing something different real fast, and sorry it was so bad before, and like me, please." It's desperate, and the audience knows it. It also, in my opinion, insults the improvisers who are already in the scene.

On the other hand, an entrance *within* the space of something already established (such as sharing a style or point of view) tells the audience (and fellow performers), "Yeah, I know it was kinda dragging a little, but it's still good, and I can add to what has been created here, and see how it bumps and lifts the energy." The performers on the stage are often grateful for this type of entrance.

Finally, before you enter, ask yourself if the scene is really that bad. It could be a perfectly fine scene in the eyes of the audience, a good, slow, two-person scene you're getting ready to mess with.

The need to get in on the funny is another reason people enter scenes. The scene isn't going badly at all; as a matter of fact, it's going great. You might find yourself thinking, "That's so funny, I wish I were in that scene," and "I wonder how I could be in that scene," and "How could I enter that scene?" and "I have an idea," and "Look, I'm entering the scene!" and then, "Why isn't the scene funny any more?" Or, "Wow, the scene is better as a result of my entrance!"

The difference between the two outcomes is *motive* and *execution.* Many improvisers enter because of selfish motives. They can't get their own work going so they want to take advantage of the funny others create. They have little regard for whether the entrance would help the scene; they just want to steal a little something for themselves. Sometimes they get away with it; often they don't. When they don't, it is usually because their motives affect their behavior in entering the scene. They may, for example, appear too eager when they enter. The audience catches this energy and the entrance loses credibility. Also, if they are too eager, their entrance is often ill timed. Sometimes improvisers can't even wait for the right moment because they are so eager to get out there in that successful scene.

The person entering might also radically change or undermine what is already working well. Talk about killing a scene dead. Yeah, that's right, pull the rug out from under something that's working great. The audience will loooove you. It's amazing to me that some people "think different" in an entrance, even if it completely changes the scene that was working great before. I really hate that.

"So, is this to say that I should never enter a scene that is already working?" No, just make sure the entrance will really support the scene and not your own ego. If you do make the assessment that you could truly support the scene, then take on a character or point of view that already exists. That's *what is going on*; and *what's going on* is what the audience is enjoying in a good scene. Add to that.

Imagine a really funny scene where two good ole boys find themselves at a museum. They are discussing how they don't understand what the big deal is. Although my example is clichéd, let's assume the scene is going really well. A third player backstage decides to enter. Here are some options (I've seen each of these many times):

1. (contrived high-status voice) "Hey you rednecks, get out of the museum!"

2. (kid voice) "Dad, mom says we have to leave now."

3. (good ole boy voice) "I don't know, I kinda like it."

4. (good ole boy voice) "Hey, I was just lookin' at the Piecassos, and they ain't much better."

5. (British accent) "Interesting painting, isn't it?"

Now what's the best choice? For my money, number 4. It's in line with what the scene is about, so the entrance heightens the *we don't understand what the big deal is about these famous paintings* concept. Number 1 suggests that the scene should stop. Number 2 is slightly more subtle, but wants to do the same thing as number 1: end the scene. Number 3 is very common. It's that need to be contrary or different, added with a little "yes, and" conditioning that makes people always go for the wishy-washy positive. (If I had a peso for every time I've heard the exact words, "I don't know, I kind of like it" in a three-person improv scene . . .) Number 5 is the improviser who is thinking, "That scene is going great. It would be really funny if I came out as a British guy" (the most opposite character and status choice). Now the scene that was previously about two guys reacting to a painting has changed into two guys reacting to a guy who is reacting differently to a painting. Oy.

Another reason to enter a scene is if you think it's gone on for long enough and you want to call an edit or get the lights to go out—to end it. This can either be a noble gesture or an annoying one, depending on the group's philosophy, the form they are presenting, and the shared experience of the ensemble improvising together. In this case the entrance doesn't really serve as an entrance, it serves as an edit—a way to cut the scene to another or for the darn lights to go out. To make this kind of entrance, pretty much do the opposite of everything I've said before. This scenario does not seek continuum, but closure. So if there is agreement of point of view on stage, enter with an opposing or different point of view. If something needs to be resolved, resolve it. If the scene's about waiting for someone, enter as the person they are waiting for. Anything to answer the why of the scene or give closure to any mystery. If you want to enter a scene to get the lights to go out, think *differently*. Even if you don't get a laugh (which you often will), you will at least manufacture enough necessary resolution energy for the lighting person to zap the lights out or for another scene to begin. If you want to do this, I stress again to think of *why* you are doing it. Is it to serve the scene as a whole, or is it for your ego?

A less devastating way to enter is to walk through or *pop in*. You walk across the stage or pop in a door or a window and say something and get the hell out quick. Whether this type of entrance is appropriate depends on the particular ideals of the group. Some groups love them; others find them disruptive. If the improvisers doing this entrance know what they are doing, walk-throughs can lift a scene, get a quick laugh, and not disrupt. If not, walk-throughs can be a dead weight.

> MAN: Excuse me miss, have you seen my monkey?
>
> WOMAN: No, there was a baboon over by the spring dress rack earlier, but no monkey.
>
> MAN: I was trying on a green tie in the men's department, and I tied up Pete the monkey by the ladies' fancy hat rack.
>
> WOMAN: (looking) Oh is that it? No, that's a sloth. Sorry, no Pete.

This scene is about the *absence* of Pete the monkey and the sales lady being okay with the fact that animals run rampant in the store.

I want to enter. If I enter as the monkey and *staaayyy* in the scene, I risk violating what the scene is about: absence of monkey. But what if I pop in and out as the monkey, preferably without the characters on stage "seeing" me? (Even if the actors actually see me, hopefully their characters won't. If the characters see me—the monkey—then the scene might shift to pointing out and chasing a monkey, as opposed to looking for a monkey that they don't know is there.) They still play *can't find monkey*. I pop in every once in a while as the monkey, get a laugh for the scene, and pop out. My entrance is *of* the scene. It doesn't squelch anything that the scene is about, it allows my fellow players to continue playing their scene without calling it up, and it adds a bit of energy and a laugh. In this kind of entrance, enter as an element that is of/from the existing scene and get the hell out.

Watching a scene, running into the scene, and tapping a person's shoulder and switching places with them as a new character is called a *tag-out*. You tag out a player on stage. The other character or characters almost always remain the same. If you want to enter and tag out someone, hold on to some element of their point of view. For example, Character A is making fun of Character B. Let's say both characters are kids in a schoolyard. Character C tags out Character A. C portrays a teacher and further mocks Character B. Character D tags out C. She is the mother of B, and mocks him even more. By tagging, the players can advance what the scene is about, switch locations and characters easily, and further the scene quickly. Sometimes it even becomes a rapid succession of one-line tag-outs based on a single theme, like little blackouts. Tag-outs can be a fun device for entering, but use them sparingly and know what you are doing and why.

IMPROVISER 1: I think Johnny the clown will be here any minute.

IMPROVISER 2: Yeah, that clown is two minutes late!

Now, do you enter the scene as Johnny the clown? If the scene isn't absolutely about *that they are waiting*, help them out with Johnny the clown. But if it is about *that they are waiting*, don't be Johnny. Godot can't show up in *Waiting for Godot* because the play is about *that they are waiting* for Godot. The three sisters can't get to Moscow.

If someone calls for a character and that character's presence would add to what the scene is about, enter strongly with what is called for.

A special circumstance: Sometimes improvisers call a character into the scene because they have nothing going on and are floundering. They get freaked out and rely on calling someone in as a crutch to save them. In this case, enter that scene with a very strong declarative character or point of view. It will be your unfortunate burden to create what the scene is about.

Be careful of entering a scene just because some random thing is referenced.

WOMAN A: Peter and I have been fighting constantly.

WOMAN B: This Kool Aid is delicious. Yes, Fred and I have been tense, as well.

MAN A: (enters, his arms outspread and yells): Hey! Kool Aid!!

This scene above is obviously about mutual trouble at home, not what Woman B was drinking.

Four-, Five-, Six-, and Twenty-Person Scenes

So often laborious are these scenes that I almost couldn't find the energy to write about them.

A typical scenario: The lights come up halfway through a show, and you find yourself on stage with four other people. One of the people is upstage left, dancing around frenetically. Two people are downstage right, standing. Another person is in the center painting. The fifth person is upstage right with a cup in his hand, looking at everyone else on stage. Now what? Who does what and when?

It's tricky. To be honest, my first reaction if I'm in this scenario is to think, "Yippee" or "Alright" in the most sarcastic manner possible. If getting it straight in a two- or three-person scene is not tough enough, imagine all of the interaction permutations in a five-person scene.

My best advice is, first of all, know what is the dominant energy of the scene. What is the most dominant thing going on in the scene *right now*? Once you've identified that, go with it. The first step, identifying that dominant energy, requires much practice and is difficult for a beginning improviser, because what seems dominant is, quite often, quite not. In the example, it might seem like the person who is dancing frenetically is the dominant energy, because she is making the most noise and moving the most. But with experience you start to learn that people who continue a frenetic movement on stage, particularly in a group scene, are in their heads, especially if they make the move and never give it a rest. The audience picks this up and *very* quickly all they are hearing is white noise. (A hint: If you find yourself in that position, always remember that you can start frenetic as your declared initiation, then stop to let the scene happen, then resume as necessary to keep the frenetic ball in the air.)

So the loud dancer probably isn't the dominant energy. How about the person observing, with the cup in his hand? Probably not. I'd bet he obligatorily "went to his environment" first and is a bit in his head wondering what's going on. The painter? Very possibly, since she is center stage and engaged in an identifiable physical activity, anchored in what she is doing. How much *how* is in what she is doing would affect whether she truly is that dominant energy. Blindly, though, I'd put my nickel on the two standing downstage right. That's where the audience thinks they will get their answers.

An audience is always looking for context: "What is the road map for the thing that I've been invited to enjoy?" When the lights come up on stage in this group scene example, the audience thinks, "Oh the lights came up, look, chaos. Oh there's someone painting. Hey, maybe those two are getting ready to talk to each other and make sense of all of this. Hey, I think I'll watch them and wait." This thought process happens in about three seconds. At this point, those two improvisers are the dominant energy of the scene.

Now, the words. When those two utter words, their words become the dominant energy of the scene. And whatever those words are, the other three improvisers will increase their chances of a good group scene if they align themselves with those words. (I know this sounds rather rigid, but if you watch some good and awful group scenes, you'll start to get a feel for this concept.)

In the example, one of the two improvisers downstage right says (in a Georgia drawl):

DOWNSTAGE A: This drought ain't gonna let up.

I suggest that everything align to that notion: *Drought, no let up.*

PAINTER: Yes, I need more blue paint for my "Ode to a Rain" piece.
DANCER: Soon, Raingoda will heed my dance and deliver the drops from the heavens.
GLASS HOLDER: I'll drink to that.

Go with that dominant energy—it's the best chance you've got in a group scene.

Unfortunately, this isn't what usually happens. Improvisers will all go a different direction or merely try to justify their own thing, or sometimes no one says anything for way too long. It may also be, in the above example, that even though the two downstage right capture the audience's attention *before* words come about, one of the other improvisers actually initiates with words. In that case, the first verbal initiation becomes the dominant energy and I'd advise everyone else to go with that.

So:

Lights up. (Pause) (Pause)
PAINTER: Soon my masterpiece will be done.
DOWNSTAGE A: We'll sell Renaldo's painting for a million yen.
DOWNSTAGE B: Yes, the buyer will meet us in Milan.
DANCER: Renaldo, you capture my dancing beautifully!
GLASS HOLDER: I'll drink to that.

Ahhh, perfect world. Unfortunately, all that I'm talking about doesn't usually happen. In reality, the person who chose loud dancing will probably be, as mentioned earlier, frenetic. Then she will have a carnival of self-judgment that puts her in a place where she is not looking for "dominant energies." The dancer is dancing and regretting the dancing and not knowing what to do and keeps dancing and blah. The guy holding the glass is probably in his head, too. He's looking at the others, trying to figure out what's going on and who's going to do what next and why. The two downstage right are going to start a scene without keeping the *whole* scene in mind, and continue on a disparate course of dialogue in their own world. Finally, the painter is wondering why she is painting and is aware of frenetic dancing and is annoyed but in her head. Then chaos continues.

Often, intermediate improvisers will realize the need to have a dominant energy in a group scene so they force it a little. I'm talking about the "Welcome to" and the "Okay everyone."

The lights come up and there are eight people on stage. A conscientious player sees this and immediate exclaims:

CONSCIENTIOUS PLAYER: Okay everyone, we have to decorate this Christmas tree for the party!

or

CONSCIENTIOUS PLAYER: Okay everyone, get in your seats because class is getting ready to start.

or

CONSCIENTIOUS PLAYER: Okay everyone, who has an idea for the campaign?

The subtext for this is, "Okay everyone, we're in a confusing group scene so let's get on the same page right now."

The "Welcome to" usually happens more as a game move in a long form. After a few two- or three-person scenes, someone will see the need for a group scene. They will then travel down stage, look at the audience, and say, "Welcome to the dog show," or "Welcome to 'Who's Telling The Truth?'" or "Welcome to (anything that declares group context and forces a dominant energy in the scene)."

Over time, improvisers become more deft in these proclamations. They learn to find a smoother way in. Instead of the literal feel of "Welcome to Science Hour," they might utter, "Last week on

Science Hour . . . " and then graduate to " . . . the lifespan of a snail. Now Science Hour examines . . . " Among new groups this, then, becomes dangerous because if that initiator doesn't get that context out quickly, the new and eager improvisers will babble and stumble and change the scene to a chaotic nothingness of tedium.

My advice to groups is to practice finding those dominant group energies together. If a group has a shared protocol, it makes for a less stupid and more coherent experience for the audience. The exposition becomes slyer, the scenes build more organically, and players more quickly realize their function in the scene. With enough practice, it's amazing to see just how quickly five or six or even eight people can get on the same page.

So,

- Practice identifying the dominant energy.
- Practice responding to and acknowledging that energy while staying true to your own initiation at the beginning of the scene.

How an improv group manages their group scene work is a sure sign of how successfully they will show up.

8 Advanced Improvisation

ools to help you improvise richer, funnier, more substantive scenes is what this here chapter is about. Sometimes I use this motto to describe improvisation: "Improvisation, always different, always the same."

Although improvisation is making it up as you go along, and there are no two scenes alike, there's a particular set of moves that people usually resort to. If I gave 100 pairs of improvisers the location suggestion of "cave," ninety pairs are going to do a scene about how to get out of the cave. Nine out of ten scenes that take place in a submarine will have at least one person raise their hands to the periscope. Hot air balloon scenes: How to get to the ground. Bowling scenes never take place in the bowling alley office, always at the alley. The hand goes up to indicate the ball in someone's hand, the person bowls, then both people in the scene look at each other to determine whether it was a strike or not. Then the other person bowls, and if people are clever they will hold one hand to the side, palm down. Air blower. If I only watched improvised scenes to get my information in life, I would think that:

The only thing you do in a *graveyard* is dig graves.
There is a guru on every *mountain*.

People at *bus stops* talk about buses, then try to seduce one another.

People at *train stations* talk about trains, then try to seduce each other.

The only thing people do in *boats* is fish.

Bakers only roll dough in a *bakery*.

Pizzas are thrown in the air at all *pizzerias*, all the time.

People are on their knees praying at all times in every *church*.

All people who work in *laboratories* are insane.

All *doctors* do is tell people that they have a short time to live.

People say "shhhh" most of the time in *libraries*.

Always different, always the same.

The reason that improvisation is often within the same general realm of choices is because people have very similar associations when they hear a suggestion. *Graveyard* brings up *shovel* and *dig*. A *submarine* makes you think of a *periscope*. Common associations. The following are ways to break that up and create uncommon, more exciting choices.

Opposite Choices

Make an opposite choice in your scene. Make a choice that seems opposite of what you think you should make. Too many improvisers go for the "appropriate" choice, or the choice that they think will be appropriately funny. If you're given *used car lot* as a suggestion, it is expected that you might immediately try selling a car to your partner on stage. Most improvisers go there. It's expected and appropriate and seems like it has potential for some laughs. Problem is, it's typical. Imagine how refreshing it might be to have these two characters as coworkers at a used car lot bitching about their girlfriends. No buying or selling, we would expect that. By making this unexpected choice we automatically create something as more exciting. We already and immediately bring it to the less mundane, and more theatrical, choice.

Now what does that do to your head? It puts you in a wonderful world of discovery, as opposed to playing out the all too familiar used car negotiation scene. Even though the audience gave you the suggestion of used car lot, hoping that you would go in to the buying/selling premise because that's how they associate the comedy as well, it's not true that that is where the greater comedy lies. By making that opposite choice for them, you immediately surprise them.

If you've seen a few husband-and-wife scenes, think about how many of the characters argue in those scenes. That's pretty ordinary. Now imagine how delightful and surprising it might be to see a husband and wife do a scene about how much they love each other, or how silly they are. When you make this quality of choice, you're putting yourself in unfamiliar territory. As that may be a little scary, it's also more exciting: for you, for your scene partner, and for your audience. It also shows up smarter. You're a step ahead of the audience if they subconsciously or even consciously predict a choice on your part, and you completely surprise them with something other. It gives you a little instant credibility and probably a better foundation for a funnier, richer, more surprising scene.

The same thing also applies to character choices. All too often improvisers bring out the same old typical expected character choices. Pirates that say "Arggh," priests in confessionals, and gay men who are effeminate are common character choices. If you are given the suggestion of *accountant*, try not to immediately go to a tax session. It would be surprising and delightful to see this accountant at an ice cream truck, then filter *accountant things* through the purchase of an ice cream cone.

Specificity

Specificity is one of the most effective tools in improvisation and easiest to do. Specificity is bringing detail to your scenes. If you watch enough improvisation, you begin to notice that many of the reactions from your audience are a consequence of an improviser being specific about something.

Not being specific is another result of fear. When we're in a state of self-judgment, we tend to be vague. I've seen many a scene start with something like, "Thanks, now just put *that* over *there*," or "*They* will be *there* soon." It's a lot safer, subconsciously, to not take the chance in naming something in detail. A scared improviser will keep

it vague so as not to impose too much, or risk that a specific reference will not get a laugh. That improviser will be nondescript and
feel as if they can catch up later with detail.

A mark of experienced improvisers is the amount of specifics
that they weave into the scene. "Thanks, now just put that red vase
over there next to the porcupine statue," or "The legislators will be at
Sonny's Deli soon." Specifics color the scene for the audience, provide more valuable information to your scene partner, expedite the
scene greatly so you don't have to go fishing for the substance, and
garner quicker and more substantial laughter or other positive reaction from your audience.

A lot of people confuse these thoughts about being specific with
my earlier rants against thinking about exposition and justification.
They feel that on one hand, I'm telling improvisers not to use a lot of
words at the top of the scene or you will cripple the scene with too
much exposition, but on the other hand I'm saying add as much
detail to the dialogue as possible. This is confusing; let's take a stab at
clearing it up.

The exposition I speak of is usually there because either an
improviser has been told to find the *who, what, where* at the top of the
scene, or as a result of not knowing what is happening in the begin-
ning/middle of the scene. Out of fear an improviser may blurt out a
string of words to explain what and why something is happening.
My advice regarding specificity assumes that the improvisers are at
the point where they will make a strong dialogue choice at the top
out of emotion or character, and then, starting in the middle, fill that
dialogue with character-embodied detail.

The top of the scene exposition dialogue sounds like, "Tom,
being my brother it's important that you and I clean this garage
before Dad gets home or we won't be able to go to the party." It's
often without strong character or emotional investment and played
nearer to the cadence of the improviser. The exposition within the
scene as a result of fear is something like, "Every time we go anywhere together you start acting crazy like this. Why don't you stop
acting crazy and let's get this raking done."

Specificity in improvisation is different. It's like this:

The lights come up and an improviser, slightly hunched, walking
downstage with a limp, says in a raspy voice, "Yeah, that was 1957,
the last time I saw Ellen in that old red barn." This isn't an improviser

confining and describing the circumstance of the scene, nor is it someone who is assessing another improviser's behavior or his own. No, this is an improviser who has made a strong character choice, is starting in the middle of the scene, and then applying specificity to his character's voice and words. The physical also becomes part of the detail, in the hunch and the limp.

Going to the environment and discovering objects that the character would use is also a means of bringing in more color and detail. How does the character put on glasses? How heavy is a cane? How big is a book and how quickly or slowly does a character open it? Specificity will bring more layers to your scene with more fully dimensional characters, and if it's important to you, more laughs.

Pull Out/Pull Back In

This is a little tip to use once you have an idea of what you and your scene are about. *Pull out/pull back in* means pull out, or go opposite the point of view you've been declaring in the scene, then pull back in to restore your original point of view in the next beat or line of dialogue. A simple example of this:

IMPROVISER A: Hurry up and get dressed so we can get to the party!

IMPROVISER B: I don't know, I'm not sure I'll fit in.

IMPROVISER A: Of course you will, you're gonna meet someone you like.

IMPROVISER B: This shirt is stupid, I'm gonna look lame.

IMPROVISER A: So there will be lame people there you can meet, let's move.

IMPROVISER B: Okay, okay, I'll give it a shot.

IMPROVISER A: Cool, let's go.

IMPROVISER B: No, I'm gonna look like a rod. I'll stay here and eat cashews.

B's point of view is fear of being an outcast at the party. He plays that point of view twice in the scene. Then, at the third beat he gives in to going (pulls out of his point of view), and the next line reaffirms his fear of going (pulling back in), thereby restoring his initial point of view.

It's a bit trick-y (I don't mean tricky, but kind of like a trick), but it does give the initial declaration more power after you restore it and provides the audience with the feeling that the scene is pushing and pulling against itself in a good way. This also helps alleviate the feeling we get sometimes that our scenes are too linear, or one-note. Other narratives do this all the time. (Oh no, here comes *The Wizard of Oz* again).

Dorothy can't get home to Kansas. Several times in the movie, though, she alters her point of view to "Now I *can* get home to Kansas," only to discover that there is yet another obstacle preventing her from going home, which restores her point of view to *the desire to go home.*

"I'm in a land called Oz and I *want* to go home. Look, a Good Witch who tells me about the yellow road, which means I *am* going home. Oops, no I'm not because of the Wicked Witch of the East, but I finally made it to the Wizard's castle, so I *am* going home. No wait, I have to kill the witch so, once again, I *want* to go home. Look, I've killed the witch so I *am* going home with the help of the Wizard. Uh-oh, the Wizard is just a man, I'll *never* get home. But he's going to fly back in the balloon, so I *am* going home. Damn, the balloon took off without me, so I'll *never, ever* get home, but here comes the Good Witch with the ruby slippers, I *am* going home, look, I *am* home. Finis."

It's a little fake-out for the audience. It gives your scene a bit more complexity. Often the restore of the point of view gets a laugh, a kind of relief laugh that you're not really abandoning your point of view, just pulling away from it for a second. Remember, though, you have to create and establish the initial point of view before you have permission to toy with it and pull away and back in.

Curve Balls

Another thing you can do once you have your scene established is throw a curve ball. By this I mean say or do something that is totally outside of the deal you have created. I know, I know, this seems contradictory to what I have said before in regard to holding on and adding to the point of view for dear life. So I'm not saying to abandon or dismiss what you have created, just throw something in the scene that's not directly related to what the scene is about and see if you can catch up to it later.

Let me try an example. Here's another scene:

A: Billy's coming over later.

B: I know, around three this afternoon.

A: He's got some bad news.

B: Some bad news for *you*.

A: Yeah, Billy's gonna tell me that mom found out about the car.

B: Tim, you're screwed.

A: Dad's gonna kill me when he sees the scratch. I'll never play another video game ever.

B: Scratch? I'd call it a fairly large scrape.

A: Do you like butterflies?

Do you like butterflies? What the hell? Obviously this scene is not about liking or not liking butterflies. It's about this person dreading his parents' wrath over a scratch in a car. Butterflies?

Isn't he bailing or changing his position in the scene? The scene continues:

B: Sometimes. Sometimes I adore butterflies.

A: Just trying to get my bike out of the garage. Should have retaped my handles. Big scratch.

B: Big scrape.

A: When I was younger, last year, I used to take a net that mom bought me and romp in the meadow and carelessly chase butterflies. Of course, that was before the scratch.

B: Yes, chase butterflies before the big scrape.

A: It's almost three o'clock.

B: You're screwed.

Ah, now it's okay. Butterflies are about Timmy's dread of his parent's wrath. He will be denied his butterfly-catching pleasure as a result of his careless action. That is indeed what the scene is about.

The improviser may or may not have known of his eventual construction of the butterfly beat as it was introduced into the scene.
Hopefully he didn't. I'm asking you not to know.

It's sometimes surprisingly fun to introduce something that is
seemingly outside the scene. The audience is taken aback for a
moment and then delighted to see its relevance soon thereafter.
Throwing a curve ball shakes the scene up and is perceived as a bold
move. Oftentimes, it also gets a yuk. I've talked about surprising
from within the scene; well, this is surprising from outside the scene
and then discovering that it is within the scene.

For this to work though, two things have to happen:

1. You need to establish the point of view, and make sure your
   audience and your partner are aware of it, as well.

2. Your partner can't freak out as a result of your strange
   offering.

In the example, it is quite clear that Timmy is in trouble. It is
also quite clear that the partner didn't wig out; he says, "Sometimes.
Sometimes I adore butterflies." The partner merely accepted the disparate offering, stayed on track, and trusted that butterflies would
weave into what the scene was about later. Imagine how the scene
would have gone south if the partner had reacted like this:

A: Do you like butterflies?
B: Yeah, let's forget about the car and the scratch and go to the
   park and look at butterflies. Let's go!

Yes, the partner has to keep a cool head and hang in there. So do
you if a curve ball like this is thrown at you. This is another level of
trust among experienced improvisers. Knowing that everything's fine
if you just hang in there and don't freak. Stay with your thing and
you'll catch up with it in a moment or two.

It's also possible to hold the scene even if the curve ball info is
never enveloped by what the scene is directly about. In this case, it's
like juggling two balls and gives the scene layers and texture. I use
the same scene as an example:

A: Billy's coming over later.

B: I know, around three this afternoon.

A: He's got some bad news.

B: Some bad news for *you*.

A: Yeah, Billy's gonna tell me that mom found out about the car.

B: Tim, you're screwed.

A: Dad's gonna kill me when he sees the scratch. I'll never play another video game, ever.

B: Scratch? I'd call it a fairly large scrape.

A: Wanna Coke?

B: Thanks, it's 2:30. You have a half-hour left in the free world.

A: Coke's lost its fizz. Maybe I should flee to another continent right now.

B: I've got twenty bucks. I don't think that will get us there.

A: I spent my last cash on flat pop.

B: You're a dead man.

As you can see, *soda pop* runs more or less parallel in the scene to the dread of doom. It doesn't take anything away from the primary energy of the scene, but adds another layer and more texture and detail to the scene. Once again, this only works if everyone is level-headed and trusts these types of offerings. You're dead if anyone freaks out and bails.

Reaching for an Object

You are in the middle of a scene. It is going well. You have a character, your partner has a character, and you both are playing a scene that is about something. For an added extra challenge, reach your hand out into the air, or the environment of the scene, and pull it back with an object in your hand. Keep playing the scene. Keep holding the object. If you are brave enough to do this without pre-conceiving what the object is before you reach, you will soon discover what it is, and it is likely that it will be in the ballpark of what your character or the scene is about. This is similar to throwing a curve ball in the scene and catching up with it later. That was a verbal mechanism; this is a physical one that involves the environment. This scary move will escalate the play and discovery of the scene. At best, it heightens what the scene is about; at worst you'll create it as an incidental object in the scene and provide color to it.

Let's say you are in a scene and you are playing a drunken clown. The scene goes on for a while and you are wreaking havoc on some kid's birthday party. You boldly reach your hand out to grab something from the air and have no idea what it is. You bring your hand back toward you but you still don't know what you are holding. You scare another kid with a threat and an insult and then take a swig off a liquor bottle. Ah, that's what that is in your hand. A fearless move on your part has allowed you to heighten the character and the scene. It might be that you already thought of creating a bottle, then you reach out for it. That's fine, and good improvisation, but I'm also inviting you to reach out without knowing what you are grabbing to put you in this wonderful but frightening state of discovery.

For added, extra-scary fun, try this at the top of a scene. When the lights come up on stage or someone says "go" in a workshop, reach your hand out into the environment as suggested before, and simultaneously say something. As always, this could be preconceived before the scene begins, but I am challenging you to do it without knowing, or instantaneously cancel your preconceived thought. This move will most assuredly snap you into a character energy that probably never occurred to you. Don't worry about figuring out the object right away; just make that verbal initiation first and foremost. With practice, you *will* be able to initiate verbally and determine the object at the same time. It will feel like magic; thank goodness it's not.

This is especially useful if you have gotten into the rut of going to your environment at the top of a scene and then standing there silently, wondering what to say, or doing the opposite—having no environment at all in your improvisation and just standing there talking. Either of these unfortunate patterns can be broken with reaching for an object.

Personal Objects and Mannerisms

I've looked closely for years for that which separates the good improviser from the excellent improviser, and I began to notice this one particular positive pattern. Many superior improvisers will create a personal object or a mannerism for themselves in the scene.

Earlier, in the section about specificity, I mentioned the value of an object for a character in regard to the content of the scene and what it is about. I would like to elaborate now on the value of the object or mannerism to give your character more substance, believability, and integrity.

Imagine a scene where an executive is standing, waiting for an elevator, talking to an employee about his marriage. The scene is good or not, who cares. Now, imagine that while this conversation is going on, the exec has his hand out in front of him, palm down, and is flicking his ring finger up and down occasionally. It becomes obvious, after a while, that the executive has a yo-yo while this conversation is taking place. It now transforms from an archetypal executive to an executive who is yo-yoing. More dimensions: a fun, unexpected choice for an executive and another layer for the scene.

A personal object provides insight into the personality of the character. And probably some more laughs. Specificity allows the audience to see a fuller picture of the characters and the scenes, and quite often is what they empathize with and laugh at. Having the courage to create this piece of business and environment will add great substance and specificity to your character.

Even if the improviser created an object that wasn't an opposite choice, like a pointer, it still adds depth to the character. This is the difference between when object-work and environment become a crutch to go to when you're in your head and when they become powerful tools for bringing more to a scene or a character.

If you don't want to use an object, then try a personal character mannerism. Human beings rarely just stand there, arms to the side or in their pockets, and talk at each other the way we often do in improv land. People have ticks, mannerisms, and other behavioral attributes that make them more individual. If you can tap into that behavior, then your characters will become more individual, as well. Think of the executive talking by the elevator; maybe he's obsessed with stroking his right ear. Fun and peculiar. He's not the ole boring exec; he's a bit quirky. A southern belle who does a little wave after everything she says is far more interesting and fun than the typical sitting-on-porch-with-southern-drawl. Audiences love idiosyncrasies in people, and that little touch on your part is a doorway to another part of the character.

Your commitment to personal objects and mannerisms for your characters has you show up in ways that you might not otherwise, breaks you out of stereotypical patterns, and creates fuller and often funnier characters. Practice at home.

Personal Variety of Energy

You're in the middle of a freestyle long form. There is no structure, so characters and scenes do not return; each scene you do is brand new. You notice that in the last two scenes you did, you were shouting angrily and standing in the center of the stage. It is time for you to do another scene. Which of the following two options would be best for you:

- Do a quiet vulnerable scene downstage right on one knee.
- Stand center stage and shout angrily.

Stupid question? You'd be amaaaaazed at how many improvisers repeat these patterns over and over, especially in long form. They repeat the pattern within the show because that's what it is, a pattern, and patterns are hard to break. Patterns are also another consequence of measured thinking and self-judgment, so improvisers go to the safe and conditioned place.

In light of this, I suggest making variety a choice when you improvise. If you are in a long form or other structure that invites different characters and scenes within a single show, keep a mental note of what you did in the last scene and change it up. If all of the ensemble members were to think that way, not only would it give each of them more variety in their performances, but it would also give the show more variety as a whole. It also gives you something to think about other than, "What am I going to say next?" "What should I do now?" and "I wish the lights would go out."

Here are some elements of variety to keep lightly tucked away. If ensembles just put emphasis on one of these, improvisation would be a more layered and entertaining experience.

- *Variety of Emotion* If you notice that you used a certain emotion two times in a row, or that the show has had a presence of one particular emotion, make an opposite choice for the next scene.

- *Variety of Volume* It is all too common to see everyone yelling in every scene in an improv show. Make sure you are always loud enough to be heard, but play with the volume so that it's not always at the same decibel.

- *Variety of Staging* Centerstage, facing each other an arm's length away, turned out to the audience slightly is not the only position in which you can improvise a scene. It's so refreshing to see someone come all the way downstage, or downstage right, or upstage by a wall. It breaks up the monotony of talky scenes and is another way to put improvisers in unfamiliar physical territory. Notice the patterns of staging in your show and take chances to break them up. This goes for vertical height as well. Standing and talking is one choice. So are crouching, lying, crawling, kneeling, and bending over.

- *Variety of Numbers* Every scene does not have to be two people, nor does every scene have to have everyone in it. Look for patterns of the same numbers and enter or exit a scene accordingly.

- *Variety of Rhythm* Improvisation has its own special rhythm, especially when it is boring as hell. Recognize and rehearse different rhythms for you and your ensemble. If a scene has a slow pace in a show, come in faster, and vice-versa.

All of these things provide for a more entertaining improvisational experience for your audience. The added extra bonus is what it will do for you. By letting the variety serve the show, you will be doing things that you normally wouldn't do and that stretch your range as an improviser.

Starting Scenes

If you are dying to preconceive something in an improv scene, preconceive the following. (With each example, know that, as always, you'll want to have a strong choice or a *how* behind it). Practice starting scenes one of the following ways.

You

Begin a scene with the word *you*. "You got the map? Good!" or "You feelin' all right?" *You* instantly puts you in the same space as your partner. Using *you*, not only affirms your partner with your strong choice, but also immediately makes your partner a part of it. This tool is also helpful if your improvisation seems a little disconnected lately.

And

Start a scene using the word *and*. The reason is probably obvious: " . . . *and* now let's crack that safe," or "*and* that's why I wanted to meet you here." Yes, *and* starts you in the middle of the scene. It cuts through boring and unnecessary exposition. After a while, you'll want your scene to always have the cadence of *and*, but eliminate actually saying the word all the time. In my examples, it would be, "Now let's crack that safe," and "That's why I wanted to meet you here." All of this gets you into the scene more quickly.

Something You Believe In

Have the first line of your scene be something that you actually believe in or believe to be true. For me, it might be, "I don't trust the government," or "The government is corrupt," or "The government often lies to us." For you, it might be something different. It is, however, something you actually personally believe in, whether it is your stand on free speech, or capital punishment, or your favorite hairstyle, or your opinion of the Cincinnati Reds. Improvisation invites us to say anything we want at all, and to bring our own voice to the stage. It invites us to do and say anything. Anything. What do we come up with? "Great party, huh?" or "What's up?"

The Opposite of What You Believe In

Begin a scene by saying the opposite of something you believe in. I might say, "The government is always honest," or "Astrology is an amazing science." This might even be better than saying something you do believe in, because representing the opposite point of view often has more impact. It is also usually funnier; ninety percent of the time, the audience is aware that you don't really believe what you are saying.

Non Sequiturs

I love Dada and non sequiturs. Perhaps a bit too much. Try starting a scene with one, and then try like hell to catch up with your initiation. "Watch that toothbrush Samsonite, the penguins grow weary over car." This usually requires a willing partner to respond to such an initiation, and I wouldn't suggest doing this in front of audiences often. It's a great way to stretch your brain and free up the words, though. It also allows great practice in fielding difficult initiations and makes it a bit easier in the future when all kinds of initiations come your way.

Scenes Without Laughs

Some of the best scenes I've ever seen are those that are about not getting laughs. When I spewed at the beginning of the chapter, "Improvisation, always different, always the same," doing scenes where you get no laughs is a way to defy this bitter slogan. Having laughs in mind when you go on stage produces a certain mindset: very product-oriented. It has you work in a particular, limited set of actions and words. The product is the *laugh*, or the need to create that laugh. This product-thinking steers improvisers into certain patterns of behavior, and the moves associated with that behavior seem to fit into a certain kind of finite set.

Alleviating the burden of getting a laugh opens up a whole new universe. Suddenly, a moment that would have been joked out is played through. All moments in the scene appear more honest, and points of view and characters are upheld effortlessly.

If the improvisers launch these scenes with high-stakes initiations, all the better. It's a joy to see the relationship of, say, two brothers where the first line of the scene is, "Sorry I couldn't make it to the funeral." If both improvisers are in agreement that they are not going to sell out the scene for laughs, that is, play it seriously without joking it out or bailing, improvisation reaches a greater depth.

An average improv scene lasts three to four minutes. A scene without laughs can last seven, never sway from what it's about, and tug and pull in every way imaginable to play itself out. I have seen and performed in scenes like this for over an hour. Practicing such scenes lets you know that you're capable of playing a character and a point of view for far longer than you might have thought. Some improvisers tell me that they run out of things to say or do in a scene. Improvise a scene for fifteen minutes without laughs, and you will learn that it's not that you can't find things to say and do in an improv scene, it's that you can't find things to say and do if getting laughs all the time is important to you. It takes trust and integrity to play this type of scene, and anytime something jokey appears, it sticks out like a sore thumb, a clunker. I talked about acting earlier; well, this is where improvisation meets acting.

Now for the punchline: These scenes are some of the funniest I've ever experienced. Yes, the laughs may or may not come as often as they do in other scenes, but the laughs produced are of greater quality. Quality? Yes, quality—a word not used very often in improvisation. Quality of funny. Since the improvisers are not improvising with the mindset of being funny, the funny has greater depth and quality. If the improvisers are playing the scene for real and keeping the stakes and what the scene is about intact, the laughs are more organic to character and relationship. They are not cheap laughs, but more intelligent, richer laughs: better laughs.

This kind of improvisation, though, can't be achieved without agreement among the players. When one improviser wants to play this way, but the partner is in a need-to-get-a-laugh mode, the partner is going to pull the rug out from under the scene every time. The improvisers need to agree *beforehand* that this is the way they'll improvise today, whether in workshop or performance. You just can't pull out a high-stakes initiation in your Bucket O' Yuks improv team and expect everyone to hold it up. Improvisation does most often crave funny, but it sure could use a dose of the honesty and integrity found in improvising scenes without laughs.

9 Advice and Guidelines for Improvisers

Talent

Why are some more talented than others? What does it take to prevail in improvisation? Should improvisation be pursued as a career?

What do you want from improvisation?

My first piece of advice is to be brutally honest with yourself about what you want. Ask yourself why you are improvising.

If you want to work in the cast of a professional improv theater company, say that, to yourself and others. If you want to be a film star, declare that. If you would like to improvise as a hobby, then have it be that. Too many people shroud themselves with false intentions when it comes to improvisation.

Improvisation has an artistic presumption that makes people think that it is wrong to use it as a tool for writing, acting, or to further a career. While in it, people think they should hold it purely as an artistic endeavor, when really, in the back of their minds, they are thinking of having a big career in professional theater, film, or television. Improvisers would get there quicker (whatever "there" is for them) if they would just be honest with what they want. Not only is that sort of falsity annoying and tacky, it is also a practical inhibitor.

Integrity is living up to what you declare, in an improv scene and in a life. Declare what you honestly want, and live that vision fearlessly.

If you do decide to improvise as a professional endeavor, know that it is just that: a professional endeavor. And like all professions, it takes time. Improvisation has tangible skill sets and indicators of progress.

It takes time to attain these skills and the amount of time it takes is different for everybody. But it at least takes years—years of experience, either on stage or training or preferably both.

You may be the funniest thing on the block, but if you don't have the technical skill set to improvise with another person, that talent will be forever locked inside, held prisoner by the common improvisation behavioral pitfalls that reside in every beginning improviser. Just one of those moves where you lose power could get you in your head and ruin your scene.

The Concept of Training

There's such a thing as too much training. If you move to a city like Chicago, New York, or Los Angeles and enter into the lovely world of improvisation, check yourself to make sure you are balancing practical performing experience with classes.

It is very easy to get swept up into the social and academic arenas and convince yourself that you're making progress. Time on stage is paramount, and if you don't have it there's only so far you will evolve as an improvisational actor. If you find yourself enrolling in your second year of improvisation class and have had limited performing experience, my suggestion is to not enroll in that class.

Take time off to assess your station in the improv arena. You will discover much and observe those around you in your situation with a more powerful, objective eye. Then your decision to take another workshop will be just that, a decision, as opposed to a weak reaction to your perception that taking another class is what you are supposed to do.

Taking time off will also help you absorb what you've learned. The improvisation training world is saturated with varying points of view and different theories, including my own. I believe that none are wrong and none are right: Every approach has helped someone at some time improve their work. That's the beauty of paying for the service of being taught information about improvisation: You get to choose what works for you. What doesn't work, assuredly, is attempting to absorb and execute all of those contradictory influences in one fell swoop. It takes being selective and using only that which helps you. And often, determining what works for you is best achieved with an absence of any influence.

Men and Women

Angry Men

Some men think that being negative all the time—on stage or off—is novel and powerful. I am here to tell you that it is neither.

Sometimes men feel they need to roll their eyes, shrug, and knock down an idea to gain their position. What they are really expressing is fear.

If you are that guy who doesn't readily support another's idea, or slices ideas to bits before they even reach a stage, save yourself some time and stop your behavior, even if you have to fake it. Even if you have to pretend to be enthusiastically supportive against your better judgement, do it. Over time, if you are at all smart and talented, you will realize the value of that support and even begin to abhor your former behavior when you notice it in others.

Being distant, objective, and negative is dime-a-dozen behavior—a reaction to fear and a defense against doing real work.

And it is, above all, boring.

Crazy Ladies

A lot of women who enter improvisation believe that if they act a little batty both onstage and, more particularly, offstage, they will stand out. Eccentric attributes will set them apart and they will excel.

Don't be a crazy lady.

Be a strong woman instead.

Be polite and economical offstage, and relentless on stage. Let the crazy show up in the improvisation as characters.

Women versus Men

"Women aren't as funny as men." "Men bulldoze scenes." "Men type women into subservient domestic roles."

For women: If you find yourself dwelling on or reacting to any of these statements, give it up. It is fruitless and powerless. As a man, I sometimes find this a difficult conversation to approach, but I can at least make the following observations.

- It is a power drain for women to give such beliefs any credence, especially if doing so affects their work on stage.
- Men joke about women not being as funny and will continue to do so. Fair or not, they do and will.
- Men don't really believe that women are not as funny, because they have enough examples of funny women that they admire to disprove the notion.
- No strong, funny woman improviser I've ever worked with gives any thought to any of those beliefs and hates when other women do.
- If women are on a campaign to change male improviser behavior, they have about as great a chance as changing the behavior of the guy they are in a relationship with.
- Men rarely go on stage thinking, "Hey, I'm going to screw over this woman and bulldoze her scene." Most often they go on stage with their own fears and baggage and look to support whoever they are on stage with in order for the scene to go well and to have a good experience.
- Men are labeled as husbands as often as women are labeled as wives.
- The weaker and more insecure the woman, the more likely she is to dwell on and react to such beliefs. Strong women improvisers are busy improvising with integrity, regardless of what is offered to them.

The Perfect Actor

Below is an excerpt from a web journal I wrote in 1996 while I was directing "Paradigm Lost," a Second City Mainstage show. I wrote it one afternoon after a particularly trying rehearsal. I have left it word for word, harsh language and all, to reflect my mindset when I wrote it. It's a list of guidelines for an actor working on a sketch/improv show. I think it applies more broadly, though.

Shut the fuck up.

In rehearsals or notes, if you don't really really really have to say anything, then don't. Some people talk for the sake of talking. This comes from a space of rightness or need for affirmation or need to be perceived as vital and intelligent. If you don't have to talk, don't. Look at what you are about to say and ask yourself, "Is this *really* supportive to what is going on right now?" If it's not, say nothing. It's so easy to whittle away a rehearsal talking bullshit. Everyone knows that ninety-five percent of what is being said will not come to fruition, yet they do it and feel a false sense of productivity when they leave the rehearsal. I've been sucked into that waste-of-time abyss more times than I'm willing to admit.

Know what you're talking about.

If you have to talk, know what is being discussed right now, and have what you have to say be relevant to that and that only. I've wasted so much time as a director wrangling tangents and bringing them back to the point at hand. I'm pretty good at bringing it back to what's up, but I don't enjoy it and it usually pisses me off.

Make strong choices.

Fuck your fear. We want to see your power, not your fear. Nobody has time for your fear. When I direct, I assume competence, not inability. That's all a director wants from an improviser in this process. To take the powerful choices he or she creates, and utilize them in the show. If I, as director, must constantly spoon-feed and suggest and coddle the actor in regard to their ideas, lines, and characters, then there's a ninety percent chance that the person is coming from a huge space of insecurity in the first place. That's the problem right there, not the idea or character or anything. The more you approach a director or other actors in this needy manner, the more you will alienate yourself from the director's power and your own. When I teach, I expect insecurity; when I direct, I expect the opposite. If you find yourself in a show and you are afraid, then fake it. Do the first three things on this list and discover that the more you are perceived as powerful, the more powerful you actually become. When I teach I have room for insecure choices; when I direct I do not. Once you are proficient in this behavior, you will have the welcome right to discuss your scene with me or another actor. The best thing you could say to me in notes is, "I'll make another choice and we'll see if it works."

Show up and be on time.
If something comes up, call. Really.

Don't be tired.
It's actually okay to be tired; most of us are when we work so hard on a show. It's even okay to say you're tired. Just don't act tired. Be someone who isn't tired. I've seen too many people say they're tired at the beginning of a rehearsal and then spend the next three hours proving it to everyone around them. Often, tired is an excuse for lazy or scared. If you find yourself saying "I'm really tired today," know that everyone is tired and that's a given and who cares and then get up on stage and be vital and engaging. Don't let tired be an excuse—nobody cares.

Don't read in rehearsal.
Don't read in rehearsal.

Don't talk about the show in bars.
If I don't believe that talking in rehearsal is very productive—then—think about it.

Try anything.
Be someone who will try anything. If you have a consideration about something a director asks you to do, speak that consideration and do it anyway. Be someone who says, "Sure, I'll try it." Sooooo many good ideas have gone to hell because an actor (or director, for that matter) judges an idea, talks it to death, and never tries it even once. It's so easy to be negative; you think you're being smart and insightful at the time, only to learn later that you're merely an asshole.

Eliminate these words from your vocabulary.
"Can't"—Oh yeah, I'll bet we can. A process is about what we can do; it's so easy and limiting to state that we can't. A powerful person finds possibility with an idea, not its limitations. Try anything.

"Should" and "ought to"—Use the word "could" instead. "Should" forces your suggestion on me; "could" offers me the gift of choice and opportunity.

Don't interrupt anyone at any time; if you do, apologize.
If you interrupt another, you are instantly telling them a couple of things:

- What that person is saying has so little value that you didn't bother to listen.
- You used the time while they were speaking as an opportunity to think about what you were going to say, which you think is right and more important.

Now what that person is thinking about after being interrupted is "He interrupted me," so they don't hear the thing you interrupted them with. Pretty effective communication, ay? As a director, I will promise to keep my eye on interrupting you if you keep your eye on interrupting me and others.

That was the original list. Here are some added things.

Don't lie down in a rehearsal.
Many people think it a harmless thing if they take a little snooze when they aren't doing anything in a rehearsal. The message you're sending is that you are uninterested in the development process of someone else's material, that you are bored and would rather take a nap. It makes people feel bad to be working while another actor is across the room sleeping.

Learn not to apologize before presenting your work.
A cast is asked to bring in an idea or a writing assignment to a particular rehearsal; there is a slight apology before each idea the cast members are getting ready to present. They come in forms like:

"I'm sorry, I didn't have much time to work on this."

"This isn't working, but here it is."

"This is stupid, I had a hard time, but . . ."

"Before I present this, I just want you to know I hate it."

"You guys are going to hate this, but . . ."

It's very tempting to offer this sort of apology and I sympathize because it's very scary to offer an idea. Sometimes, the thought of being rejected or scoffed at is overwhelming, so you want to protect yourself by letting everyone know beforehand that you share their soon-to-be negative view. The reasons I'm suggesting getting over this behavior are:

- It's a waste of time. It takes real time out of every rehearsal to wait for everyone's apologies.
- It gives you permission to be mediocre. Every time you sit down to think of an idea or write something, you have the out that it is allowed to be mediocre because you are going to apologize for how bad it is. What if the conversation were, "I'm going to create something that warrants no apology because it is good and I'm proud of it" and you wrote from that mindset? You would then give the idea the time it deserves and not be content until it was to your satisfaction.
- It makes you look weak. If you apologize every time you present an idea to the director and the other ensemble members, then they will come to expect you to produce mediocre work.

Present your ideas proudly. They are your creation; you needn't apologize for them.

Work in the present, not the past.
Some people, when asked to bring in an idea or writing for a show they are working on, drudge up material they worked on in an earlier show. I'm not hard and fast about this, but I do think it's a bad practice for an improviser to get into. Every rehearsal process has a collective, creative sensibility comprised of all of the actors and the director and the experiences and times that they live in. That's the marvel of creating ensemble sketch comedy: It comes from that ensemble's voice. Material created outside that process sticks out as

foreign and contrived, not organic to that process. It also shows up as a crutch to the person bringing it in, suggesting that the ensemble member can't live up to the growth and challenges of that particular rehearsal process. Learn to create from within a process.

Don't meet as a group without the director.
You will screw up your show. I don't care if the person can't direct-dial, don't meet and discuss the show and the problem without the director. If this happens, there is no going back. It is the beginning of the end; the show will lose its power and will suffer on opening night or the next time it is performed. Learn to gently confront the director as an individual or a group. If there is a producer, meet with him or her. Know that discontent with a director or other ensemble members comes in waves, so give it a little time and see if the wave subsides. It might. If not, then confront; don't meet outside.

Ask permission to give another improviser a note.
If you really must give a fellow performer a note, ask their permission first. "I noticed something in that last scene, would you like to hear it?" or "May I tell you something I observed last night?" Ask permission to give the information. Then, be okay if the answer is no. Be okay if they are not in the space to receive your information. Reflect on times when people have offered you notes and how it made you feel. Respect that space and don't take it personally.

Don't give other improvisers notes.

If you must give a note, don't, don't, don't do it during a show.
This almost always infuriates the recipient. Wait until an appropriate time, like never. Or at least until the director has offered notes; the director may cover your issue.

Jump on stage with enthusiasm.
If a director says, "Let's get on stage," do it with power and enthusiasm and speed. Why? Because the sluggish, "Do we have to? I'm tired" approach sends a message of indifference and affects your work. It says that everything you are about to do on stage you will approach with less than your best. It will permeate the work you do with the precious little time you have on the stage, where ninety percent of the work that will appear on opening night happens.

Sit near others.

What the hell?? Yes. In the rehearsal room, sit near the other ensemble members, not apart. Survey the room, and if you find that you are sitting noticeably farther away from the group than they are to each other, move in closer and sit with the group. This sounds so stupid, but it isn't. Alienation comes in many forms. Sitting far away is a psychological tactic of being the objectifier, the guy (usually) who is "with" the ensemble, but who will also take on the "responsibility" of objectifying it. Often the culprit is not even openly aware that he has this behavior. The effects are subtle but powerful. Let the director be the eye of the group, the one who is objective. Your responsibility is to work powerfully as an individual within an ensemble. So be with the ensemble at every opportunity you can. Sit with them.

Shower.

Auditioning Guidelines for Improvisers

An improvisational audition can be one of the scariest experiences on this little planet.

I remember my auditions and how out-of-my-mind frightened I was. Everything, for about a week before the audition, was amplified in a surreal way. The mornings of these auditions were even more terrifying. Everything was magnified: Details that normally had little or no importance suddenly took on grand proportions.

Getting dressed was huge. "Should I wear a suit to give myself a professional actor look?" Or "Maybe I'll wear a t-shirt for that 'Hey I just walked off the street and aren't I funny' effect." Or "Maybe I'll dress up in a thin tie and a sharkskin suit. No, no, a too-long striped tie and red Converse shoes." Or "Maybe I should dress exactly like John Belushi."

Eating was another thing. "Should I eat at all? Maybe something light. No, something heavier and get a nap in."

Arriving at an important audition is exactly what it feels like to walk to your own execution. Scary, buzzing, nervous, doomed, fighting for confidence. Friends you drank with the night before suddenly become polite adversaries. The way that everyone around you acts and the way they are dressed become hugely intimidating.

Fear. Fear. There are so many people around; very scary. Walking into the theater is a nightmare. The auditors look bored and intense and uninterested from the moment you walk in. You already feel screwed by the time you walk on stage. You see one of them take a sip of coffee and that is very important all of a sudden, very aggressive and intimidating. It wouldn't normally be, of course, but at an audition everything seems amplified and constructed to kill your audition.

Here are some ways to ease the pain, not just for an improvisational audition, but for any audition.

First of all, the most important thing that you can remember is this:

Although it looks like the auditors are indifferent to you or maybe even don't appear to want you to do well, the opposite is, in fact, true. They not only want you to do well, they are *dying* for you to do well.

There is nothing they want more. That's why they are there, to find people who do well, and it might as well be you. It gets so boring, watching group after group improvise poorly, because the improvisers are so freaked out. Anything that appears to be a strong choice or a risk is highly refreshing. Truly, auditors want nothing more than to see you show up well.

And how do you do that? Well, here are some tips.

- Don't acquiesce to the energy in the room.

The vibe in the audition room is usually quite somber and intimidating, not the best place to cut loose and play. You must resist the temptation to yield to that energy. Great improvisation is not possible if you decide to give in to the tense, judgmental feeling in the room. Great improvisation is only possible if you play, and unfortunately in an improvisation audition you have to manufacture that feeling in spite of the atmosphere. It is difficult, and most people give in and become measured and stilted. If you want to have a successful audition experience, snap into play regardless of what it feels like you *should* do.

And remember, the auditors truly want you to be successful. They do not purposefully set up a tense audition environment; it just comes with the territory. It will always be that way and you must play. Easier said than done, that's for sure.

- Snap into a strong choice when someone says, "Go."

(Have you heard this before?) Allow yourself to think all the horrible and haunting thoughts you want a week, a day, minutes, seconds, and the nano-second before you improvise in that audition, but when an auditor gives the signal, leap into a strong choice. It won't feel like that's what you should do, but *do* it. Pierce through the molasses feeling of the audition and surprise everyone with a strong, engaging choice.

- If you are asked to state your name, do so slowly without affectation and without trying to get a laugh.

I've seen people say, "Hi, I'm John Belushi—just kidding." Just say your name. If you are asked to say a little something about yourself, do so truthfully. Don't make up stuff about yourself to get a laugh. If the truthful thing is funny, so be it, but don't invent anything for a laugh—it will surely be transparent and look contrived.

- Speaking of John Belushi, don't dress like him.

(Many have.) Dress nicely. The jacket-long-tie-red-tennis-shoes-jeans thing is so very tired, at least in my opinion. Dress for a Sunday afternoon spring wedding.

- If you know one of your auditors, don't acknowledge them unless they first acknowledge you.

Walking in and saying, "Hi Bob, how have you been?" puts Bob in an uncomfortable position and works against you because now Bob has to appear unbiased. Above all, after you audition, don't hang around and strike up conversations with the auditors. Get out and go have a beer.

- Show variety.

Sometimes an improv audition is an audition for a group that will perform both improv and sketch comedy. Sketch improv requires a range of character and emotion, so show that in the audition. You don't necessarily have to plan it out, just be aware of it during the audition. If you find yourself playing only one energy in one scene, switch up the character/energy for the next. So many times I've heard, "She's good, but is that all she's got?" Show that it isn't all you've got. Show a range for a sketch comedy audition.

■ Take an acting class—or four.
A lot of improvisers come from the "My friends told me I am funny" school of performing and deem acting as unnecessary or pretentious. In a sketch audition, acting skills are an asset. Many can improvise on the same level, so acting gives you a rare edge over the other improvisers, especially if you're asked to do a cold reading. If you want a real edge in a sketch comedy audition, know how to act.

■ Prepare for an audition by auditioning.
Auditioning itself is a learned skill, and many improvisers just don't have enough experience in it. An auditioning actor has many fear thresholds, which can only be overcome by experience in auditioning, not by auditioning for that one big thing once a year.

Often, people who have gotten to the point of not giving a damn whether they work somewhere or not, ironically, get hired. The reason for this? They have eliminated the importance they place on the audition. You see, if you posit your audition as crucial for your career and you must get the job or you will die, you will walk into the audition with a huge burden. It's difficult to find a sense of play with that baggage. Improvisers who arrive at a place in their lives where it just doesn't matter don't carry that burden. They leave themselves open to play, which has them show up as smart and funny. I'm not attempting to diminish the importance of the audition, but only trying to shed light on one of the many self-sabotaging psychologies at work before and during the improv audition.

Common Patterns

Finally, I would like to mention some patterns that show up in an improv audition. As always, I'm not saying don't do these things, I'm just saying that the following things often appear in auditions by people who seemingly think that what they are doing is novel.

■ Beginning at the beginning
Because of fear and measurement, a lot of improv scenes in an audition start with unfamiliar relationships and beginnings of conversa-

tions. Things like, "Hey, what's up?" and "So, how's it going?" indicate two characters with no familiar past getting to know each other in a strange setting.

If there is ever a time to assume familiarity with your partner on stage and start in the middle of a scene (" . . . so I finally told her the truth."), it's in an improv audition.

■ Sex

Improvisation is the only place on earth where sex is boring to me, particularly in an audition. Scenes about sex in an audition almost always show up as a consequence of fear, and it's frighteningly transparent and not unique. Gay, straight, whatever—these scenes are usually not so funny and certainly overdone.

■ I love

I mentioned this improv syndrome earlier, in speaking about justifying and making assessments in a scene. The "I love" thing shows up a lot in auditions, once again, out of fear. So many scenes start with:

> "I love playing baseball."
>
> "I love kite flying."
>
> "I love being in a factory."
>
> "I love working at the zoo."
>
> "I love tax time."
>
> "I love ticket taking."
>
> "I love going to the game with you."
>
> But rarely
>
> "I love you."

■ Physical contact

Whether it is strange touching, kissing, or hitting, it's probably inappropriate. Even if you know the person you are improvising with, the auditors don't know that you know them. You might be surprised by how many people slap each other in auditions. It's always disconcerting for those watching.

- Hands in pockets

Basic, but worth mentioning. A very typical pattern for people in fear is putting their hands in their pockets. Not only will it reinforce your fear, but it will also limit you physically.

Summary

These guidelines are not offered to make you overthink the audition, but lofted in the air as something to lightly keep in mind. The last thing I would want is to provide you with more "don't do this" information and put you in your head. Read and forget and remember and forget and play.

Improvisation and the Second Law of Thermodynamics

I'd like to explore the energy of an improvisational scene as it pertains to the second law of thermodynamics. The following is probably, but not necessarily, a metaphor.

Often we speak of a scene's *energy*. Is that a word we throw around to describe such things as pace, loudness, stage presence, and so on, or is the energy of a scene real? We say, "Pick up the energy in that scene!" or "We lost our energy in that last scene." Energy, energy. If an improv scene is a closed system, and the energy we speak of is real, then the scene must adhere to the laws of physics. Two laws of physics are the first and second laws of thermodynamics. Does a stupid improv scene adhere to the first and second laws of thermodynamics? Let's find out. And if it does or doesn't, who cares? Let's find out.

First of all, we need to know the definition of *energy*. *Energy* is *the capacity to do work.* What is *work* in this definition? *Work is a force on something moving it a distance.* Work = force times distance ($W = fd$). I would guess that right now you're getting into the "Oh my God, there's an equation and my brain shuts down and I hate this stuff" mode. Equations are like that, but just take a look at it. Throw a poodle off a cliff. Throwing a poodle off a cliff is *work.* You apply a *force* to the poodle and it travels a *distance.* In a moment, gravity, another *force*, takes over and pulls the poodle to the earth, another *distance*, shattering its manicured body. Work = force (your throw) × distance (how far the ill-fated poodle travels). W = fd: easy. So *energy* is the capacity to apply a force to something and move it a distance. Easy.

Now let's look at the relentless laws of thermodynamics. The first law is better known than the second.

First Law of Thermodynamics

Energy can never be created or destroyed, only transformed.

This means that there is only so much energy in the universe. You can't create more and you cannot, under any circumstances, destroy what is there. The First National Energy Bank of the Universe has one set amount of energy in its account. The energy can change from one form to another, say from solar to electrical, but the total *amount* of energy never ever changes.

"You can't win," people often say of the first law. No matter what you do in an exchange of energy in this universe, you will never ultimately come out ahead, because a greater amount of energy will never be created. Another way of stating the first law is that there is a *conservation of energy* in the universe. Energy, or the capacity to do work (which is a force moving something a distance), is not created or destroyed, it is *conserved*.

Now you know the first law of thermodynamics.

Before we travel to the second law, I want to introduce another equation, $E = mc^2$. Along with the conservation of energy in the universe, there is also a conservation of matter. Matter can never be created or destroyed. Einstein's famous equation shows the relationship between energy and matter. The E in the equation stands for *energy*. The m stands for *mass*. The c stands for *the speed of light*. *Energy = mass times the speed of light squared*. The speed of light is a constant. It never changes. No matter what the circumstances in the universe, the speed at which light travels never changes. That speed is 186,000 miles per second. So the equation $E = mc^2$ says that the energy that any object in the universe possesses is the object's mass times the speed of light squared. A beer can has this much energy:

E = (mass of beer can) times the speed of light squared. If you do the mathematics, the amount of energy in any object (its *mass energy*) is astounding. This equation is that simple and that incomprehensible.

We see no visible effects of the energy contained in the things around us, so it doesn't seem to make much sense. Think of any piece of matter in the universe, say, a thimble, having an insane amount of energy reserves, but there is never a withdrawal from its energy bank, and there is never a deposit to its energy bank. The thimble has a huge reserve of mass energy that just sits there like a hidden Swiss bank account. Is this crazy and vast amount of mass energy ever released from matter? Yes, but rarely. An example of mass energy release is found in nuclear bombs and nuclear power. One of our only rare glimpses of this energy is the tremendous amount released in a nuclear event.

Because the speed of light, c, never changes, there is always a direct correlation between energy and mass. Energy = mass × a constant (the speed of light squared). Just as there is conservation of energy in the universe, so there is a conservation of mass; the correlation between energy and mass stays equal. The first law.

("Excuse me, I really just want to improvise.")

The Second Law of Thermodynamics

In a closed system, entropy will always increase over time.

Let's break down that sentence. First, a *closed system*. There is some controversy about the definition of a closed system among scientists, but for our purposes, let's say that *a closed system is any system of interacting things that you define as such, that has no interaction with other things, outside itself.* So the solar system is a closed system that contains the planet Earth. Not much, except for gravity and the occasional asteroid, interacts with the sun, the Earth, and the other planets in our solar system. It is pretty much a closed system. The Earth itself, however, would be considered an *open system* because the sun greatly affects it, yet is outside of it. Here on this planet, we can define smaller closed systems. Never perfectly closed, but enough so for a discussion of thermodynamics. An egg, an engine, a cup of hot coffee, a car: A closed system is a system that can operate in and of itself, without any outside energy source. You may say, "Well, you have to put gasoline in a car, and that's from the outside." Yes, it's true, but I'm speaking about once the gas is in the car; the car becomes a closed system. It no longer needs to exchange energy or matter with anything outside of itself to function. It is then closed. So, back to the second law.

In a closed system, entropy will always increase over time. What is *entropy?* Entropy is often equated with chaos. Entropy is not chaos; chaos is often the result of entropy. Entropy, quite literally, is *waste heat.* Heat is a form of energy, and entropy is *waste heat.* Waste heat is heat that is emitted into the universe, *never to be used in the closed system that it was emitted from* again. Entropy is just waste heat energy.

So.

In a closed system, entropy, or waste heat, always increases over time. *Always increases over time.* Always. No matter what the energy system, over time, waste heat will escape into the atmosphere, never to be captured again.

("Seriously, I just want to do a couple of funny characters.")

Here's an easy example of the second law: I make an Irish coffee. I get distracted by a friend asking me about improv and forget I had an Irish coffee sitting on the bar. The Irish coffee, previously hot, begins to cool. It does this on its own. Entropy, or waste heat, emits from the hot coffee/whiskey pleasure into the atmosphere, never to be recaptured by that particular Irish coffee again, and thereby cooling the Irish coffee. The coffee could be given energy (heat) again from an outside source, but the original heat energy was dispersed, at random, into the universe as waste heat. That's another way of stating the second law:

Things tend toward cool. A glass of water doesn't just heat up on its own. It needs an outside source to add energy to it, and if left on its own it will tend toward cool. The biggest example of this in our world would be the sun, which will tend toward cool and burn out in a few billion years. We on Earth live off the entropy of the sun.

Here's a more immediate example of the second law: I finish my fourth single malt scotch at a bar and leave the glass on a table. In a stupor, I get up to leave and accidentally knock the glass off the table. My hand and gravity are the forces that combine to send the glass to the floor. The glass breaks. So what happened? The force of impact broke some of the molecular bonds of the glass, causing it to break. When those bonds are broken, the heat energy that used to hold the glass together is released in the form of waste heat. That waste heat energy is dispersed into the atmosphere, never to be recaptured by the glass. As a result, the glass remains broken. This is why entropy is equated with chaos. The result of the release of waste heat in the scotch glass causes disorder for the glass, or chaos, and the energy necessary to have the glass again be the glass it once was, is gone forever. Yes, you could glue the pieces back together to restore the glass, but you are really adding another energy to create mended glass, not recreating the original.

This is what things tend toward—order to disorder—because of the second law of thermodynamics. Broken glass on a floor does not spontaneously become a scotch glass, but a scotch glass is just waiting for the release of energy necessary to become broken. Everything on our planet tends toward disorder, including you. We fight the second law every day by remaining alive. No matter what we do, we tend toward disorder as we grow older and older. The second law is why car tires wear out, cigarettes burn, and dead poodles decompose.

This is also why a perpetual motion machine can never work. Throughout history, many people have tried to create a machine that, once set in motion, will eternally function on its own without any additional energy input. This machine is impossible, because the parts of the machine will interact with one another, or the molecules in the air, creating friction. Friction is a form of waste heat dispersed from the machine, never to be recaptured by it. A perpetual motion machine will eventually stop working, which is another definition for the second law.

Of the first law, as I mentioned earlier, people often say, "You can't win." Of the second law, people say, "You can't even break even." No matter what the system, a percentage of energy will always be given off, tending toward that system's disorder. It takes energy to maintain order, but the universe doesn't prefer it. An ice cream shop left empty and unattended for 100 years will become disordered. A cigarette will burn and never become that cigarette again, a universe will cool and reach equilibrium, and a dead poodle will decompose at the bottom of cliff, never to recapture its lost energy and become that poodle again. The second law.

The Thermodynamics of Improv

Now let's create an analogy (or a reality) with an improv scene and the second law of thermodynamics. First of all, it's important to define the closed system. Remember, a closed system is a system that has no external input of energy other than what is included in that system. So let's say we define the improvisational theater itself as the closed system. The whole room, once the audience is seated and the improv show is about to begin, will hopefully have no *external* energy inputs. Its *internal* energy inputs are:

- The light hitting the stage
- The audience, with their quantity and their reactions (such as coughing or laughing or clapping)
- The air conditioning and heating system
- The improvisers
- Sound energy (voices)
- Kinetic energy (improvisers' movement)
- Potential energy (lack of sound and movement)

Notice that these are also the primary factors that determine the success of an improv scene. All these sources of energy are being thrown into a scene. If *energy* is the capacity to do work, and *work* is a force applied to something moving it a distance, what is the thing that our closed system is moving forward? In this closed system, the theater, what is moving? What work is being done?

The scene itself, or what the scene is about.

That's what we're moving. That's what we put all of our energy into when we improvise. We create what the scene is about and put all of our sound, movement, lights, and audience reaction toward moving the scene forward. In a comedy scene, the audience adds real energy with their sound of laughter, fueling the scene farther. In a dramatic scene, the audience's concentrated stillness provides potential energy, which enhances dramatic tension. All of these energies are directed at the intangible, yet agreed upon concept of what the scene is about.

This is truly the *engine* of an improv scene. We often speak of "driving a scene" and "a scene that loses its gas" and "cranking it into fourth gear in that last scene." We put gasoline in a car to provide energy to an engine to move a car a distance. As improvisers, we speak and move to provide energy to *what the scene is about* in order to move the scene forward.

Our biggest goal in our quest to move a scene forward is to *reduce entropy*. We battle against the second law, attempting to *reduce wasted energy*. We strive to have all our lines, movements, character choices, and environment choices go toward what the scene is about, and nothing else. Anything other than that is wasted energy. Unlike a car, which already has an engine, we have to create our engine—what the scene is about—out of thin air. And though it's not tangible, it is real; like pistons we must fire the engine in order to propel the scene and have it move forward.

In an automobile, this is all that the pistons do: gain energy from the combustion of gasoline, allowing the engine to turn the crankshaft and move the car a distance. Imagine if the pistons of a car *sometimes* fired to move the car and sometimes didn't. Perhaps they fired and the explosion went into the air, or other times they fired and the car went in reverse at random, or other times they fired and they added a force to an engine of another car. Inefficient work would have been done to move the car a distance. Waste heat. As a matter of fact, this is what automobile manufacturers do all the time: seek to create cars with better fuel efficiency. They work to battle the second law, in order to minimize wasted energy and maximize fuel efficiency. (In countries other than the United States, anyway.)

As improvisers, we are the pistons of the engine of the scene. We must be able to create that engine, identify it, and do our damndest to add energy to it and it only. Yes, waste energy will disperse into the atmosphere, but we must do all we can to minimize it.

You may have seen a scene in which an improviser played a particular point of view for two or three beats, and then changed her mind and went with another point of view. You just witnessed a dispersal of waste energy. The piston misfired. Perhaps you've observed a scene where two improvisers glance back and forth at each other in silence for eighteen seconds in fear. You can feel the energy drain out of the scene even before the engine has been created. The audience can feel it also, and they unwittingly contribute to it by their reaction, or lack thereof.

Maybe you've witnessed a scene that starts out well enough, everything seems aligned, and then it just doesn't go anywhere or it keeps revisiting the same territory over and over again. Once again, you can feel the energy drain. Every wasted line or break of character or going to the environment with little purpose or bailing on what you created is the emission of waste energy for your scene.

Doing nothing or doing the same thing over and over in an improv scene is not even good enough: *entropy will occur over time.* The second law of thermodynamics doesn't care. It will take wasted energy from your scene whenever it can. Being all over the map in an improv scene is also not good enough: disorder will occur, the scene will break down. We need to focus on what the scene is, add our energy to that, and let the audience add theirs.

In improvisation, we don't have much time. Everything we create in a moment is true, and everything is about that truth and that truth must be fueled with our energy *now* so that we don't let ourselves waste too much energy in time, allowing our scene to reach disorder.

I am not suggesting improvising quickly, just succinctly. For example, a scene could be about *not* doing something. In that case, *not doing that thing* is where you want to put your energy. Imagine a quiet scene with two people on the thin ice of a pond; if either of the two characters move or speak too loudly, the ice will break. *The potential for the ice to break* is what the scene is about, and all the improvisers' energy must go toward that.

Whatever the scene is about, once you lose the energy of it, you can never get it back. When we say we *lost the energy of the scene,* we really did, and it ain't ever coming back.

Thermodynamics means the dynamics of heat, or what happens whenever heat energy is exchanged. Improvisation involves all different kinds of energy exchanges, and anytime there is an energy exchange in this universe, the laws of thermodynamics are lurking in the shadows. The second law is just waiting for the molecules of the scene to break, dispersing waste energy into the universe at random, never again to be recaptured in that particular form.

11 Exercises to Do at Home

Many resources for teachers and students of improvisation include exercises for a classroom setting. So I thought I'd provide some improvisation exercises you could do in the privacy of your own home.

I've done a lot of exercises by myself in my home, and almost all of them seem silly at first. That's okay. After a while you will condition yourself to just snap into it. (Sound familiar?)

These exercises each have their own area of focus, but by merely *doing* them you'll gain commitment and initiation skills. Have a bit of fun.

Some strong advice:

Do the exercise first, then read its purpose!

The first set of exercises are about thinking quickly and jolting your mind around.

Dada Monologue

(*Dada* means *hobbyhorse*. Dada was an early 20th century art and literature movement based on deliberate nonsense. Dadaists wanted to "destroy art and replace it with nothing." They replaced it with something, but the something was nothing because it made no sense.)

Launch into a Dadist monologue, one that doesn't make any sense. Look at an object in the room you are in right now and start by saying that object's name. As you talk, try not to stay on any idea too long and to make sense of nothing. I'll do this right now and write it as I go. I see a candle, so:

> Candles are dogs when books tell a story of peanuts from heaven. When I was only seven dollars I went to my own factor brush, see? No one knows my father knew his cat was a green in the Texas town of pig boy. Do you understand the flypaper jolly feet? I'll bet your desk wheel knows me.

The second you start to make sense, change it up. In my example, after I wrote *jolly*, I immediately thought "giant," but that would have made too much sense so I changed it up.

Purpose
This exercise is excellent at freeing up random associations in your mind. It jogs your mind and wakes it up to possibilities you may have not considered. I sometimes do this as I'm walking to the theater to improvise. It brings to light fun and absurd thoughts: different tools to associate with while improvising, as opposed to the limited range of associations we usually have.

Word Association

Look around the room and see an object. Say the name of the object out loud, and *without pausing*, immediately begin to talk about that object. You could describe it, or perhaps more favorably, let it spark an association about an experience you've had with it. After about ten seconds, interrupt yourself by saying the name of another object out loud and *without pausing* start to talk about something associated with that new object. Do this as long as you like, but for at least ten objects.

Purpose

This is about teaching yourself that you can literally talk about anything because you can relate to more than you may have thought.

If you want to advance this exercise, don't rely on objects in the room but come up with disparate words off the top of your head. As with the objects, say the word out loud (e.g., "ocean"), and *without pausing* launch into a story or association about the word. *Bible, puppy, envy, frog gigging, cigar*. Really make the words different.

I ask you *not to pause* before you start talking because that's a good way to practice talking and catching up with yourself. In the beginning, people will often say the word out loud, then repeat the word to give themselves a buffer, then launch into the association. Try to avoid repeating the word.

Gibberish

Gibberish is nonsensical, non-English babble.

"Gloshka moruque a mot?"

"Tikatow too."

"Nocka nu nu."

That's gibberish. You can do it right now. Do it. Yes, now, start speaking gibberish.

Good.

Now that you can do that, choose a character with a particular point of view: whatever you want. Speak a line of gibberish from that character's energy. Then respond, in gibberish, with a character who has a very different energy or point of view. Now you are doing a gibberish scene.

Purpose

Speaking in gibberish allows us to eliminate the importance we usually place on words. Notice that in gibberish, your emotional life is awakened. Practice a few gibberish scenes and you're practicing to put the *how* into your improvisation, that is, *how* someone says something versus what they say.

The following exercises are about unthinking character creation.

Solo Character Switches

Put a chair in the middle of the room. With a clock, watch, or timer in view, begin a character monologue. At the end of thirty seconds, without any pause at all, switch the character to something completely different. I say *without pause* because I want you to have to catch up with your own talking and throw yourself off guard. You can do this for as long as you want. I have had students do it for up to an hour with sixty characters, each a minute long.

A variation of this is to write down character types and put them in a hat, such as "Russian dancer" or "crazy clown," and alternate between drawing a character type from the hat and making it up on the spot.

The chair in the middle of the room is there to offer variety of physical space. Have some of the characters on their feet and others sitting. Variety of character is the key. If you notice your last two characters were quiet, make the next one loud, for example, (This is a physically strenuous exercise, just to let you know.)

Purpose

This is about stretching your character skills, along with fearlessly initiating scenes. If you can condition yourself in this way, you'll get there quicker when you improvise with a partner. "Get there" meaning establishing a strong point of view and strong initiation.

Character Interview

Put questions that you might ask another person in a hat. These questions may vary from the personal to the workplace variety. Some examples might be:

"Where are you from?"

"What's your favorite ice cream and why?"

"What is a sad moment in your childhood?"

"What are you reading now?"

Write about fifteen questions. After this, sit in a chair, hat close by, and launch into a character monologue. Let this go for about a minute, then "take questions." Pull a question out of the hat and answer the question as the character.

Purpose

This exercise will help you put yourself on the spot as a character. The more you vary the questions, the more you'll practice stretching yourself so you can better handle any variety of elements that come your way in an improv scene.

Styles and Genres in a Hat

Put twenty styles and genres in a hat. These can range from film noir to action film to horror to romance. Start a character monologue and let it get on solid ground for about thirty seconds. Then pull a style or genre out of the hat. Have your character immediately be affected by the style or genre.

Let's say your character is a mechanic. You then pull *romance novel* out of the hat. The mechanic character could immediately begin talking about his *passion* and *love* for cars. After you feel comfortable with simple styles and genres, you could challenge yourself and throw in book authors and playwrights. (This might require that you become more familiar with authors and playwrights, which is a good thing.)

Purpose

Styles, genres, and the distinct styles of well-known authors and playwrights are often used to inspire improvisation. Your understanding of them will not only give you more tools to use as a scenic improviser, but will help you with an assortment of improv games as well. Learning different styles and genres also raises your reference level, and brings more theatricality and variety to your work.

Sound to Dialogue

Stand and make a sound, any sound. Let that sound slide into a character's dialogue. Improvise for around ten seconds as that character, then make another sound and slide it into another character. For example, I make the sound, "Ohhhhhh." Then I let that slide into a character: "Ohhhhhhhkey-dokey, I want a biscuit!" or "Eeeeeeeeeeeasy does it! Don't come any closer."

Do this for about six hours. No, do this for about two minutes.

Purpose

This is a great way to stretch out your voice and arrive at characters you didn't even know were in you. It's also a great way to train yourself to make a vocal initiation in a scene, and force your brain and mouth to catch up with your initiation.

The following exercises are about the physical: body and space.

Environment

Stand in the middle of a fairly empty room. Now, without thinking, reach out in the air and grab some imaginary object. It's tricky, but truly challenge yourself not to preconceive the object. The second your hand hits that object, let it inspire you to choose what it is. Then go ahead and use the object.

So, for example, I just reached out and grabbed something. I didn't know what it was until I reached out and when I saw my hand I was inspired to think, "torch." So now I have a torch in my hand. I start walking with it as if I am in a dark room. If the object were an oven, I might open and close the oven door. If I found that it was a banana, I might peel and eat it.

After you have used it, set down or leave that object, taking note of where it is. Then immediately imagine another object that is somehow associated with the first object.

So in my example, I take the torch, put it in a torch holder, then pick up a wine bottle.

Next, find a third object that might be appropriate to the first two. In my example, I have a torch and a wine bottle, and I find an old trunk. At this point, you might get an idea of where you are. Let that inspire you to find a fourth object. In my example, I feel like I'm in an old cellar, so now I find an old dress.

Continue until you've created about ten objects. For bonus points, see if you can revisit all of the objects you have created in this environment. Congratulations, you just created an entire world by reaching out your hand.

Purpose

This is a great way to practice creating environments. By beginning with nothing but the act of reaching out, you will learn to immediately come up with something, and you'll find over time that doing so is not so scary. You will also find you can create a whole environment, regardless of whether a location is offered as a suggestion for a scene. Further challenge yourself by creating an environment while in character monologue but not talking about what you are doing. From the very first second you reach for the first object, begin talking.

Body Parts

Walk at random around a room. Think of a body part, such as a nose, then lead with that body part. By *lead*, I mean give the nose presence: Stick out your nose a little and walk forward. After a bit, switch the body part and give that presence. For example, give your right shoulder presence and continue forward. Keep doing this until you have gone through every part you can think of—head, nose, chin, toes, left knee, wrist, chest, pelvis, shoulder, left ear. You get the idea.

Purpose

When you lead with a body part, you will discover that it actually makes you *feel* differently. It gives you an instant character. This is a great tool to help you make character choices that wouldn't normally occur to you. After you do the exercise a couple of times, do it over and make character sounds that feels like the character you have embodied. Then, as a third challenge, actually bring each character to words: Start talking in character.

Breakfast

Lie down on the floor. Without words, create a character (perhaps using the body part exercise) who wakes up, gets dressed, and gets ready for the day. Have each moment evolve, learning more about the character as you go along. How does that character brush her teeth? What kind of clothes does he wear (which might depend on his occupation)? Is the furniture in the bedroom brand new, old and shabby? Where does she live?

After getting ready for the day, have the character prepare and eat breakfast, again paying attention to details like preparation, speed, and type of food, given the character. After breakfast, have the character do what he would do to leave the house or apartment. Does she need a coat? Does he need car keys or a bus pass? Does she wear a hat? Details help you create a physical world that tells the character's story. Take your time with each object discovered, committing to its weight, texture, and use.

Purpose

This is about character discovery through committing to a detailed environment. You will spend time with each element of the environment, using the location and objects within it as a tool to tell your character's story. I am bad at this exercise, but have seen others have much success with it. I hope you are one of them. With the same attention for detail in mind, you could set up infinite scenarios for characters in subsequent exercises. Have your character arrive at work, go to the park, and so forth.

Object Monologue

Write the names of twenty objects on slips of paper and put them in a hat or bowl or bucket or Tupperware. Launch a character monologue of your choice. Every once in a while, grab a slip of paper and glance at the object written on it. Continue the character monologue as you integrate the object into the scene: not so that you focus on it or talk about it, rather that it is incidental or used to accentuate the content of the monologue.

Purpose

More practice with creating an environment and with reaching out into the environment while improvising the scene. A common mistake for beginners is merely talking about the environment or the object they are holding. Practice in having the environment be incidental is invaluable.

Next are some exercises to improve your scenic improvisation.

Scene

Sit in a chair in the middle of the room. At any point, launch into a dialogue with another character. Immediately respond as the second character and continue the scene. With your first attempts at this, you may become self-conscious and tempted to stop. Overcome this temptation by timing yourself and making yourself continue for thirty seconds. As you practice, the length of time you're comfortable with may increase.

This exercise is easier if you make the two characters as distinct as possible. Whether or not you'd like to physically shift your body during this dialogue is up to you; if it helps you, go for it. I think of this exercise as a vocal-mind-momentum thing.

Purpose

This exercise challenges you to keep two balls in the air at once. At first, the exercise tends to bring about simple question/answer scenes. As you practice, your scenes should get more complex, giving each character a distinct point of view. In improvising a regular scene with two improvisers, it's tempting, if not probable, for one improviser to think of what to say next while the other is talking. While this is often inevitable and not even bad or wrong, taking on both of the characters, as this exercise forces you to do, allows you to know the world of truly being in the moment. It's great to know that you can do that.

Scene with Emotional Shift

This exercise is the same as the previous one, but each character has a different emotional base. One character might be angry, the other giddy. Practice playing the extremes of emotions, as well as subdued expressions of emotions. Some improvisers will yell at top volume when they are playing anger; others will lock the emotion in and quietly whisper through clenched teeth. Depending on who you are, you may tend toward extreme outward expression or hold it in and let the emotion out a bit at a time. Both are valid ways to express anger, but practicing the one that is less comfortable for you is truly beneficial.

After you feel confident in this foray, challenge yourself by declaring the more gray emotional states, like jealousy, indifference, and angst. For a greater challenge, improvise a scene by yourself where the characters are distinct, but share the exact same emotional state.

Purpose

Anything you can do to stretch your emotional range while improvising is valuable. The emotional states you can pull from, and the way that you play those emotional states, will inform many an improv scene as to what it's about and the characters' points of view. Most people stay within their own comfort range when it comes to emotion; opening that up now will bring you great rewards later.

Scenes of Status Shift

Improvise a scene by yourself, as before, but instead of emotion, shift between high and low status. Start with a distinctly high-status character (e.g., a professor) and a distinctly low-status character (e.g., a student).

As you create more scenes, muddy the line between statuses until you create two characters with nearly the same status. Even though you are improvising a scene alone, watch as the two characters vie for the upper hand in the scene.

Purpose

Many, many, many improvised scenes are about status. It's a powerful thing to know how to play. Status and point of view go hand in hand. Either a character is trying to get more status or is fighting to hold on to their status or lying about their status. Status is often what the scene is actually *about*. Practicing all the permutations of status will help you when you come across it in a scene. Improvisers also tend to make the same choice: either high or low status, each time they improvise. Analytical people tend to improvise in high status, often objectifying what's going on in a scene. (I used to be this guy, so I'm really aware of it.) For example, one character says to another:

"Let's go play in the sandbox."

The other character might say:

"OK, Billy, I'll bring a shovel."

or *objectify* the experience by saying:

"You play in the box and I'll watch."

Objectifying is often clever, but it sets you outside the scene, commenting on the experience, as opposed to playing within the experience. The objectifier usually takes on a high status role. Some people find more strength in creating higher status for themselves in scenes; others get a lot of mileage from low status. The ability to play from either status, or everything in between, is the best possible tool to have. Think for yourself which status extreme you tend to play more, then challenge yourself to play the opposite.

Heightening

Stand. Start a scene, with words. Doing only one character's dialogue, heighten your own character's point of view. Pretend there is another character speaking gibberish. Constantly put fuel on your own fire, adding to and heightening the energy or point of view you have already created. Pause for the other improviser's "dialogue." For example:

ME: That's a cool-looking dog.
Pause
ME: Three-legged dogs are rare.
Pause
ME: Damn thing's name is Rexy?
Pause
ME: It's standing next to a cat with one ear.
Pause
ME: Never seen a green cat and a three-legged wiener dog.
Pause

So you get the idea. You just keep improvising your half of the scene, bringing more and more to your initiation.

Purpose

Even though improvisation usually involves two or more people, improvisers must learn to bring heat to their own initiations. This exercise will help you maintain and heighten your own thing, while sustaining your ability to filter anything else that happens in the scene, or anything your partner says and does, through your character.

Read a Character from a Play Out Loud

Read plays, read plays, read plays. I said it before in regard to styles, now I'm saying it in regard to improvised characters and scenes. What better place to learn about scene construction and character attributes? Now, not only read a play, but also read a character out loud. Don't worry about how well you are doing with the acting, just read it. Notice, as you are reading, how the point of view of the character (or in acting terms the *superobjective*, or *want*) heightens and flourishes and is unwavering. The playwright does this on purpose. In improv, as I have said thirty times, you must create the point of view yourself.

Purpose

I can't tell you enough how valuable reading plays is. (Have I told you enough?) People ask all the time, "How can I get an edge in improvisation?"

Well, right here is the start, because my answer is always, "Acting skills."

That's the edge. That's it—seriously. Professional improvisation companies are quite often not so improvisational, but more sketch. You have to play roles. That's an acting job, first and foremost. I've seen so many good improvisers go bye-bye because they lack acting skills. In addition, if you can think this far ahead, after all the improvisation—the long form, the games, the professional sketch comedy troupe—continued success always comes back to acting. So learn how to do it. Start this afternoon.

Film Dialogue

Turn on your television. Turn off the sound. Find a movie. Improvise the characters' dialogue.

Purpose

This is fun and usually funny. The biggest thing this exercise does for you is force you to keep going. Improvisers often feel as if they've reached that threshold where they can't do or say anything else. In this exercise, you must keep talking as long as the film characters talk. At first, you may take only one character's dialogue, but I invite you to work up to improvising all of the characters for a half hour or so. It's hard work. Once again, notice how characters' points of view remain intact and are heightened throughout. After you do a film or two, try sitcoms, the news, cooking shows, and so on. Enjoy.

Next are some miscellaneous extra bonus exercises.

Write an Improvised Scene

Sit down at your typewriter, writing desk, or word processor. (Sit down at your computer.) Now, write a two-person scene, but do it in this way:

- Get a timer and allow yourself five minutes.
- Never ever ever stop typing. (It is hard and your fingers will be tired at the end of the five minutes.)
- Do not censor yourself or self-edit or worry at all about punctuation or spelling. Just keep typing fast.

To go even faster, name your characters A and B. You should hit between three quarters of a page to a page and a half in five minutes, depending on how fast you type.

Do not worry if the scene is bad.
Do not worry if the scene doesn't make sense.

Purpose

This is a writing exercise as much as an improv exercise. If you truly do this without corrections and without stopping, your mind and words will go places that normally wouldn't occur to you. This opens up a different, creative side to your mind that can't emerge if you are measuring what you are doing while you are writing. I really like this exercise because it just gets your ideas out there furiously. You can always go back and apply structure. After some practice, you may amaze yourself with how you can differentiate and heighten two different characters' points of view, at the same time acknowledging and heightening what the scene is about. But don't stop typing.

Songs

I do this exercise way too much. I think there's something wrong with me.

While at home or strolling down the street, improvise a song. This is quite scary for some people; for me it is a disorder. How do you improvise a song? Seriously, just start singing. As with improvising a scene, you will discover the melody and what the song is about all at the same time. Rhyme or not, but over time learn to rhyme. Also, practice not commenting on a bad rhyme. Just keep *in* it, and don't pause or comment *on* it. (The reason I say this is that in performance, improvisers often condition themselves to laugh or comment on the evidence that they can't rhyme, as opposed to finding the fun in rhyming well. Unfortunately, they often get laughs, which reinforces the behavior.)

Purpose

If you keep improvising, there is no way in hell you will escape having to improvise a song. You can either maintain the conversation with yourself that you're not a good singer or can't improvise music and be in pain, or you can start learning how to do it well today. (Psst, wanna 'nother edge in improv? Start taking singing classes this afternoon.) This exercise will also help you if you're called on to improvise a poem.

Counting to One Hundred

Stand in the middle of a room. Pretend you are a great speaker and that 5,000 people have gathered to hear you speak. Instead of words, though, use numbers. Start counting out loud, pretending that the numbers are a great speech. Take your time and continue until you reach 100. Provide as much variety in the presentation as you can, sometimes asking questions, other times making declarations. Use emotional variety as well. Know that you are coming to the end of the speech around count ninety, and use the last ten counts to provide closure to the speech.

Purpose
This hones general performing skills by allowing you to play with commitment, emotion, and variety without the burden of thinking of words to say. It is also a drill in finding the importance in the words you say. This is a basic performing idea often lost in improvisation: the notion of actually having what you or your character says be important.

Dance

Turn on some music you like and dance. That's all, dance. And really commit to it. Don't make fun of or comment on the fact you are dancing; as you do when you are asked to dance socially, really dance.

Purpose
I can tell a lot about the way improvisers improvise by the way they dance. Sometimes, just by the way they walk. Most improvisers are not in touch with their bodies, especially men. They often believe that improvisation is all about the words and the funny, not about the body or the physical. If you can get to the point where you are comfortable with seriously dancing, you will overcome a lot of the fear and give yourself permission to be a physical being in an improv scene. Today is as good a day as any to really let yourself go and escape the bonds of your perception of your physical self. Dance. Really. You will learn something about yourself.

It will also come in handy if you ever get a date.

Notes on Good Acting

Choose a good film with good acting, one that you have seen before. Choose a lead actor in the film. Now, watch the film, with only that actor's acting in mind. Take notes on what makes that acting good. Write down what surprises you: the kind of builds the actor creates in his dialogue, why she took that pause, and so on. Do this with two or three films and compare your notes. Look for a pattern in what *you* believe to be good acting.

Purpose
Studying what people do when they act or improvise well adds more options and tools for an improviser. Everyone likes different things in acting, and academically identifying what those are will help you "own" what you find effective, making those techniques more tangible and applicable. The reason that I suggest watching a film you've already seen is to lessen the chance of getting caught up in the story and increase the chances of looking at the acting with scrutiny.

Non-Fiction Summary

Read a piece of nonfiction, a chapter or so. Here are some example topics:

How to wire a three-way switch

What is the event horizon of a black hole?

How was the safety pin invented?

What was the War of 1812 about?

How does a water heater work?

Then, as a character, summarize the concept to an imaginary person. As always, don't think ahead, just put the book down and start talking. I hesitate to say, "As a character, *teach* an imaginary character the subject matter," because *teach* is such an undeservedly naughty word in improvisation. But I probably mean that.

Purpose

First of all, you're reading about something other than improvisation, which is a great thing. Second, you are improving your reference level and mind. Third, you are learning to incorporate that reference level into your improvisation by weaving it into a character monologue. Fourth, you are learning more about adding specificity to your work, which adds richness and substance and more laughs. Fifth, you are remembering the ideas you read about by putting yourself in the position of describing them out loud.

Exercise

Exercise.

Purpose

You don't have to be a bloated, pasty, pale, liquor-soaked viscous jelly blob.

Exercise.

12　Annoyance

*S*ince 1987 I have worked with many people to create what has become a wonderful place called The Annoyance. Here's a bit of history about this theater and production company.

On September 10, 1987, I sat with a group of friends around a table at an Italian restaurant talking about slasher films. After a while, we got the crazy idea of producing a blood show for Halloween, which was only a short while away. We set our goal for opening October 10, exactly one month ahead to the day.

In the next frantic four weeks, we pulled a show out of thin air. We created skeletal beats for the show—more or less a parody of contemporary gory horror films—learned about stage blood, and created and perfected our effects. Through improvisation, we honed the beats and developed the characters. Borrowing from Alfred Hitchcock, our stage blood consisted of chocolate syrup, water, and red food coloring. Some of the stage effects included a nun getting drilled in the back of the head, a bimbo getting her tongue ripped out, and a policeman having his intestines removed. With a freshly painted white set, *Splatter Theatre* opened on October 10, 1987. After a chilling original opening song performed by a nightclub singer character, several deaths turning the white set blood red, a real meat puppet intermezzi, and many laughs, *Splatter Theater* received a standing ovation.

Nobody knew at the time that we were launching The Annoyance Theater. We were just doing a show. As a matter of fact, Annoyance wasn't even our name yet. We called ourselves Metraform. *Metra* because we were performing a long-form improv show at a theater on the fourth floor of a great music club called The Cabaret Metro, and *form* because we were performing other various original improv forms at another venue. It wasn't until we formally rented a space in 1989 that we came up with The Annoyance. (Metraform didn't seem like a very compelling name for a subversive comedy theatre, so a few friends and a bottle of tequila yielded The Annoyance as the name of the theatre itself, with Metraform remaining as our company's name.) As The Annoyance became The Annoyance, Metraform went away.

Since then, in five different locations, The Annoyance has created over 100 shows, comprised of improvisation, sketch, full-length plays, cabaret, and full-length musicals. Hundreds of people have performed in Annoyance shows, and you see many of them today on stage, in films, and on television.

Our flagship show, *Coed Prison Sluts,* was created from improvisation. It ran for eleven years, the longest-running musical in the history of Chicago. Because of the content of *Coed Prison Sluts* and other shows at The Annoyance, the theater has become known for its subversive language and themes. (Such titles as *Manson: The Musical, Tippi: Portrait of a Virgin,* and *That Darned Antichrist* helped fuel this notion.) Shows like these were not so much born from the desire to be radical, as they were a consequence of the invitation to everyone in the ensemble to do whatever they wanted on stage. Our work has always been uncensored. (The only censorship is self-imposed, and the criterion of that censorship is whether or not the content fulfills the mission of the show.) Under the umbrella of the same invitation to freely create on stage came *The Real Live Brady Bunch,* a re-enactment of Brady Bunch episodes on stage; *God in a Box,* an exploration of commercialism in America; *He Who Says Yes,* a tribute to the music of Kurt Weill; and original Christmas, improvisation, and sketch shows. The Annoyance has made its mark mostly from being the first improvisational theater to devote itself to creating full-length plays and musicals from improvisation, but is always open to any type of show. The Annoyance also scored a first in Chicago for committing itself to performing multiple original shows per week. At one point, we had thirteen different shows running a week.

In 1999, The Annoyance branched into production and formed Annoyance Productions. In that year Annoyance Productions released its first feature film, *Fatty Drives the Bus*, through Troma Pictures, on video. Currently, The Annoyance strikes a balance between live performance and production, with continuous projects on the slate for both.

Along with the creation of shows, The Annoyance has provided training in improvisation since 1989. As our approach to improvisation has evolved, we have been able to provide a healthy alternative in the study of improvisation. Highly individualized attention has become The Annoyance trademark: Students leave our program with a better sense of themselves on stage and with strong tools to navigate through an improv scene. Although The Annoyance has great respect for long form and games, we focus our training on *the scene itself*, and the individual people and elements that make up the scene. Like our creations on stage, The Annoyance training program is uncensored and free of traditional improv rules, providing an encouraging environment in which to improvise.

The Annoyance ensemble has changed over the years, but they have and continue to be the funnest, funniest, and finest people I have ever met. Visit us at *www.annoyanceproductions.com*, or drop by our current location at 4840 N. Broadway, in Chicago. Stop in sometime and have a beer.

IMPROVISE.

SCENE FROM THE INSIDE OUT

MICK NAPIER

For more than 20 years of directing, teaching, and participating in improvisation, Mick Napier has watched thousands of scenes. His experience has led him to continually question why and how scenes work or don't work and what one must do in order for a scene to be successful. In this book, he takes an irreverent but constructive look at the art and practice of improvised scenes. He covers such topics as

- two-person scenes
- group scenes
- entering scenes
- techniques to achieve richer, more layered scenes
- auditioning
- solo exercises for practice at home.

Napier also challenges the conventional wisdom of the *rules* of improvisation, examining what's behind them and how they came to be in the first place.

Get helpful, tangible guidelines for bringing strength and direction to your scenes. Just *Improvise*.

Mick Napier is the founder of the acclaimed Annoyance Theatre/Annoyance Productions, as well as Resident Director and Artistic Consultant for The Second City. He lives in Chicago.

www.heinemanndrama.com

ISBN 0-325-00630-X

9 780325 006307